IMPERIAL CHISLEHURST

TO MY WIFE – A FAIR MAID OF KENT

Elizabeth I knights Sir Thomas Walsingham: Chislehurst's village sign was carved by
John Easden in 1953 to commemorate the Coronation of HM Queen Elizabeth II.
The author designed the sign.

Funeral procession of The Prince Imperial, from Camden Place to Chislehurst's Catholic Church in 1879 – taken from an original print.

IMPERIAL
CHISLEHURST

The story of a Kentish village
by

T. A. BUSHELL

BARON
MCMXCVII

FIRST PUBLISHED BY BARRACUDA BOOKS LIMITED,
BUCKINGHAM, ENGLAND 1974

SECOND EDITION 1980

& IN THIS THIRD EDITION
BY BARON BIRCH FOR THE BARRACUDA COLLECTION
FROM QUOTES LIMITED 1997

PRODUCED BY KEY COMPOSITION,
CHEYNEY & SONS, HILLMAN PRINTERS (FROME)
& WBC BOOK MANUFACTURERS

ISBN 0 86023 579 3

CONTENTS

ACKNOWLEDGEMENTS

The author wishes to acknowledge the great help he has received from so many residents, past and present, during the twenty-five years that he has been gathering material for this history. Among the many who have thus helped are the following:

Lady Baker;
Mrs. J. Bareham;
Mr. A. Battle;
Miss T. Battle;
Mr. L. Bayman;
The Misses O. & L. Bristol;
Mr. J.R. Campbell Carter;
Miss Carnell;
Mr. N. Cole (Knowstone, Devon);
Mr. Frank Draper;
Mr. John Easden;
Mrs. A. Field;
Alderman Mrs. A.L. Gunn, J.P.;
Mrs. R. Hall;
Mr. William Lash;
Mr. J.T. Ledner;
Mrs. V.M. Linscott;
Major J. Marsham-Townshend;
Miss Meers;
Miss Helen Nussey;
Major A.J. Oldendorff;
Mr. S. Peters;
Mr. F. Pierce;
Mr. C.A.R. Richards (Bromley);
Mr. & Mrs. J. Stockford;
Mrs. G. Streetly;
Mr. W. Tapsell;
Mr. & Mrs. A. Turner.

The co-operation of the Kentish Times is also acknowledged in allowing the use of certain of their photographs, and for their permission to reprint in the early chapters of this book, material that originally appeared in serial form in the Chislehurst Times, in 1959, 1960 and 1961.

Poynings,
Chislehurst
SEPTEMBER, 1974

FOREWORD

by Air Chief Marshal Sir John Baker, G.B.E., K.C.B., M.C., D.F.C.

I have known Tom Bushell for the past twenty years. It did not take long for me to realise that he was not only the best historian in his knowledge of the background of Chislehurst itself, but that he also had an unique ability to link together the varying parts of our County of Kent—whether he was speaking impromptu or before a formal audience.

I came to know his talents and amazing erudition more intimately when I was invited to become President of the Chislehurst branch of the Men of Kent and Kentish Men. At that time Tom was our Chairman, and continued in that more modest office after being elected a Vice-President of the Association.

I am only echoing the words of all those who have known Tom and his charming wife, over the years, when I say that there is none better qualified to put on historical record the story of Imperial Chislehurst.

John Baker

PREFACE

For all its proximity to London, Chislehurst is a village, and a Kentish village at that. Its origins are shrouded in mystery, though the Saxons gave it its original name. Once a Royal manor, later home to Emperor and Prince, it has played host to more than one Queen of England. Today it is commuter country, yet retains its identity and its rural appeal. The people of Chislehurst, whether from old established families, or the newer housing estates share this in common; they love their village and they like to know why it is the way it is, the better to appreciate its many charms. They will find in this book the people, places and events of the past that together tell that story.

Clive Birch
Autumn, 1974

9

SONNET TO A KENTISH VILLAGE

Sharp stones, and timber yet unhewn
Concealed the flow'ring glade,
When conqueror's swift and seeking blade
Sang development's first tune.

Kings ruled, queens came, lords stayed,
And perhaps the bard pursued his muse
While church and manor took their dues,
And commoners thronged the cockpit's shade.

From foreign shores in saddened flight
Came empire's outcasts, sore afraid;
Since then both greed and war have laid
Their claims to changes great and slight.

This place in honour so rehearsed
Is peace, is home, is Chislehurst.

C.B.

INTRODUCTION

Three quarters of a century have elapsed since, in 1899, there appeared The History of Chislehurst, by Webb, Miller and Beckwith. In that same year, in the Chislehurst hamlet of Prickend, I was born.

History is made every day, and research constantly adds new facts to old. For example, Dr. Leslie Hotson, discovered tucked away in the Public Record Office, Queen Elizabeth's pardon of Ingram Frizer for his part in the death, in 1593 of Christopher Marlowe. That window shed further light on Chislehurst history and led indirectly to the events of May 1, 1956, when at the instigation of another American, Calvin Hoffman, the tomb of the Walsinghams in Chislehurst's old church was opened to see if there might be found there the missing manuscripts of the Shakespearean canon *in the handwriting of Marlowe.*

Our three earlier historians knew relatively little of Marlowe, but must have been better informed as to the Imperial Family of France. Their reticence on this subject may have been because the Empress was alive, or because the Emperor's earlier escapades might not then have made acceptable reading.

Eugenie has passed to a greater reward and times have changed, so that now the story may be more freely written, not to rival Webb, Miller and Beckwith so much as to supplement their work.

The Imperial connection covered a mere eighteen of the thousand years of local history, but nonetheless we are known as Imperial Chislehurst, and this seems an appropriate enough title to distinguish this record from that of 1899.

Lastly, this history is part topographical, part chronological, dealing where appropriate with some streets and the green in sequence, so that the reader can recreate the past for himself or herself, walking through historic Chislehurst.   T.A.B.

11

SAXONS AND NORMANS

Chislehurst began as a clearing in a wood. It was a stony place. We are not surprised therefore, to find that our Jutish fore-fathers called the place "Ceosol Hyrst"—a pebbly wood. Earlier this century the commons had far fewer trees upon them than they have now. The pebbles were everywhere visible and many of them were of a purplish hue. They are now almost all covered by many years' fallen leaves.

No record remains of the Jutish settlement. Our earliest record is a charter of King Edgar dated in or about the year 974. King Edgar made a grant of land in Bromley to the Bishop of Rochester, and the royal lawyers defined the boundaries of the land concerned and so gave us our first mention as Cyselhyrst.

All historians up to recent times had thought that apart from natural features, Chislehurst retained nothing from that early period 1,000 years ago. But restoration work on the west wall of the Parish Church brought the surprising discovery that the west end of the nave was of Saxon origin and not Roman. The flint walls of the church were under repair in 1957 when a small portion caved in to reveal a blocked window-opening of a type usually found only in Saxon buildings. Such windows had an equal splay externally and internally. The newly discovered opening is turned with rough flints. The inner splay remains blocked. Being immediately over the large modern west window and not being centrally placed, no purpose would have been served by re-opening it internally. It is thought that the original opening would have been unglazed. It has been left as found, except that tiles have been placed to form a sill to prevent weathering. Incidentally, the wall is rather thin; another indication of Saxon work. The probable date is about the turn of the 10th century, shortly before the coming of the Normans. Nothing else remains of that early church beyond this wall, as far as we can tell.

The royal charter of 974 refers to the king's boundary at Chislehurst, showing that from the earliest times this was a royal manor. It also explains why Chislehurst does not appear in Domesday Book. That famous work was compiled mainly for tax purposes and the Commissioners had no need to record places which were already in the king's hands.

It also explains why Chislehurst had no manor house. The kings, holding perhaps 1,000 manors up and down the country, could not reside in each of them as lord of the manor. But it may be argued that Chislehurst has a manor house. This appellation (with that of two nearby roads) dates back to a certain G.H. Baskcomb who, in the 19th century, wished to sell his land for development and thought that a nice name would improve the value.

That the church in Chislehurst was well established by the year 1089 we know from the grant of the advowson (presentation to the living) which was made by Gundulph, Bishop of Rochester, to the monks of the Cathedral Priory in that year. Gundulph was one of the great builder-bishops.

A little after this time, perhaps about 1150, the font was made. On coming to Chislehurst as Rector in 1846, the Rev. F.H. Murray found this font completely encased within a wooden box. When this was removed the stonework was found to be in pieces. It has since been restored.

The only companion in date to the font is a simple Norman bracket somewhat crudely carved in the form of a grotesque face on the east wall of the Scadbury Chapel.

The West end of Chislehurst Parish Church, showing the tiny Saxon window in the gable. (Courtesy of F. Draper)

14

SCADBURY

The village of Chislehurst was a royal manor, and as such was held by a succession of monarchs down the ages and sometimes by other members or supporters of the royal family. Among the latter were Joan, the Fair Maid of Kent; Warwick the Kingmaker and the Countess of Richmond, mother of King Henry the Seventh. There is no evidence that any of these distinguished people ever visited the place other than the first Elizabeth. In 1611 the Crown sold the Manor of Dartford (of which Chislehurst was an appendage) and the latter was acquired by Sir Thomas Walsingham and has been held with Scadbury ever since.

The name of Scadbury is said originally to have meant "the robbers' strong-place," but by the 13th century it had become a respectable manor. Not that the de Scatheburys, the first known owners, were lacking aggression. In 1311, when William de Craye was away with the King at the Scottish Wars they came down the hill to Pauliness Cray, assaulted the missing knight's servants and took away his goods.

In the following year Sir William de Craye complained that this same John de Scathebury, and John his son, had assaulted him in London. The result of these pleas is not known. The last John de Scathebury died about the year 1346 and it is probable that the lower front panels of the present Walsingham tomb originally formed part of his monument, displaced no doubt during the rebuilding of the church by his successors. These panels do not exactly fit their present situation and they are of a style of decoration belonging to the 14th century, before the Walsinghams came to Chislehurst.

After several changes of ownership within a short period, the Manor of Scadbury was purchased in 1424 by Thomas Walsingham, a Vintner and a Citizen of London. By this purchase began the association of the Walsingham family with Chislehurst, which was to last over 200 years. They bought Scadbury as a country estate while still retaining their house in London, in the parish of St. Katherine's by the Tower. Even in those far-off days, Chislehurst was a favourite place of residence for City merchants. It so remains to this day, but their clerks and typists now live here too. The second Sir Thomas Walsingham succeeded his father in 1459 and, although no documentary evidence is available, it seems more than certain that he provided the money for the rebuilding of Chislehurst Parish Church, during which the present north aisle and tower were added, together with the north arcade and the wooden rood screen that forms the Scadbury Chapel and separates the chancel from the nave. All these are consistent with the architectural style of the year 1460. The Walsingham tomb, which is made up of panels of different date, was probably erected in 1581 which is the date appearing on its upper part.

The oldest identifiable monument in the church is the indent from which the brass has long since been removed, to Constance Dryland of Davington, wife to this Thomas. She survived him nine years, during which time she took another husband and became Mrs. Green. The indent shows that this lady, who died in 1476, had a butterfly headdress. In order to show it successfully on a brass, the face of the lady has been turned to one side instead of looking upward as was more customary. Although this brass is lost, the inscription is on record. The second oldest identifiable monument in the church is a brass, happily still intact, to the Rev. Alan Porter, Rector of Chislehurst from 1446 to 1482. This is in the place of honour within the recess in the chancel known as the Easter Sepulchre, and this provides further confirmation that the church was rebuilt in his time.

16

It seems that the moated manor house of Scadbury, little more than the footings of which remain to-day, was also built at this time. It was a large building, the lower part of brick and the upper storey of timber corresponding in part to Ightham Mote: in fact, the latter was used as a model for the representation of old Scadbury carved on the Chislehurst village sign. No picture or drawing of the house exists but the present owner has an inventory of the entire contents, down to the smallest detail, as they were in 1727. This document contains nearly 2,000 words and provides us with the names of all the rooms and various parts of the old house, which included a Great Gate, Great and Little Brown Parlours, Great Hall, Kitchens, Pantries and three surviving cellars. Upstairs were eight principal bedrooms, including Queen Elizabeth's room over the Great Parlour. There were, in addition, numerous dressing rooms, closets and furnished passages. Also within the moat were "privy gardens," a brewery and a dairy. The whole was approached by a drawbridge, the corbels of which may still be seen.

This was the house inherited by the next Walsingham, James, the son of Thomas and Constance aforesaid. His son was Sir Edmund, knighted at Flodden Field for his gallantry in 1513. In 1520 both of them rode forth from Scadbury in their full panoply along the drive to St. Paul's Cray Common, to join King Henry VIII on his way to the Field of the Cloth of Gold.

Sir Edmund Walsingham was for 22 years Lieutenant of the Tower of London, throughout which period he enjoyed the full confidence of his Majesty King Henry VIII. It must have been a difficult task, as the Lieutenant was directly responsible for the many important prisoners of that period and all too often had to conduct them to their execution on Tower Hill. Bishop Fisher, Queen Anne Boleyn and Queen Catherine Howard were among them.

Sir Thomas More, who was received at the Tower Gate by Sir Edmund, addressed him thus: "I assure you, Master Lieutenant, I do not mislike my cheer, but whenever I do so, then throw me out of your doors." When he came to the scaffold, Sir Thomas, finding it a very rickety structure, used those words known, we suppose, to most Englishmen: "I pray you. Master Lieutenant, see me safe up, and for my coming down, let me shift for myself."

Sir Edmund died in 1549, but the Corinthian tablets over his tomb and the inscription beginning "A Knight sometyme of worthie fame lyeth buried under this stony bower . . . " were not erected until 1581, which date is clearly shown on gilded figures on the monument. For over 400 years Sir Edmund's helm and sword hung above his tomb, surviving fire and tempest, peace and war, until, in 1952, they were stolen in the dead of night. In that year an unguarded ladder led up to a temporary platform under the roof within the Scadbury Chapel, which was under repair. Nine years went by and then I received a visit from a young man who said that he had just completed his national service in the army in Cyprus and whilst there had read, in the Kentish Times, scathing remarks on this theft. He knew the thief and would return the stolen articles on a promise of anonymity. That given, the helm and sword were pitched through my door that same evening by the same young man. It was quite clear that he indeed knew the thief well. They were intact except for the tiger crest on the helm, "which had fallen to pieces". This is not the end of the story, for lord of the manor, Major John Marsham-Townshend undertook to have them cleaned and restored and they remain in his custody.

During the long period of Sir Edmund Walsingham's sojourn in the Tower of London, Scadbury seems to have been occupied for a time by his brother William, to whom was born there a son, later to become Sir Francis Walsingham, famous Secretary of State to Queen Elizabeth. During this period also, Scadbury was obviously leased to the Bacons, for (Sir) Nicholas Bacon, later Lord Keeper, was born here. He was the father of the famous Sir Francis Bacon, Lord Verulam, to whom some attribute the works of Shakespeare.

It is quite remarkable to find so many names associated with the (so called) Shakespeare authorship controversy also associated in one way or another with Scadbury. Christopher Marlowe actually lived here from time to time. Roger Manners, Earl of Rutland, is claimed by some as an alternative candidate. He married Elizabeth daughter of Sir Philip Sidney and granddaughter of Sir Francis Walsingham. Finally, the present owner of Scadbury descends from the de Veres, Earls of Oxford, one of whom is claimed as the author of the Shakespeare canon.

When Sir Francis Walsingham was no longer living at Scadbury, he kept in close touch with what we might call our branch of his family and drew his cousin, the fourth Thomas Walsingham, into the web of State. England, a small country whose total population was at that time less than that of modern London, was beset by powerful enemies and had always to be on her guard. Thus the astute Sir Francis maintained regular contact with the Continental courts, his cousin Thomas being one of those whom he employed on secret missions overseas.

Employed on similar missions was a certain Christopher whose many absences from his college at Cambridge raised doubts in the minds of the authorities; doubts which the young Marlowe, sworn to secrecy, could do nothing to dispel. When the time came for him to receive his degree of Master of Arts, the university proposed to pass him by, until an edict from the Privy Council reminded the authorities that they had no knowledge of the great services which the absentee had rendered to the Queen and nation. The degree was immediately granted. Perhaps Thomas Walsingham and Christopher Marlowe were employed upon joint missions. If so, what more secluded place than Scadbury in which to lay their plans? If not, they are likely to have met in the course of their duties. Thus it came about that the richer and more influential man became the patron of the struggling poet.

Marlowe was born at Canterbury in the year 1563/4, a few weeks earlier than another poet and playwright was born at Stratford-upon-Avon. He was the son of relatively poor parents, but of a brilliance of mind which secured first a scholarship to the King's School in his native city, and in due time another which took him to Corpus Christi, Cambridge.

Before he left the university he had become the most brilliant poet and playwright of his time. To quote Sir Henry Irving: "It was Marlowe who first wedded the harmonies of the great organ of blank verse which peals through the ages in the music of Shakespeare. It was Marlowe who first captured the majestic rhythms of our own tongue and whose mighty line is the most resounding note in England's literature."

How often, or for how long, Marlowe was at Scadbury we do not know. That he attended our parish church we are in no doubt, for in one of the very few remarks of his that have come down to us (apart from his written works) he complains of the sermons at Chislehurst. It is more likely that it was the preacher whom he disliked, for the Rector was then the Reverend Richard Harvey, a contemporary of the poet at Cambridge, with whom he did not get on at all well.

How far Chislehurst influenced Marlowe's work we do not know. Was he thinking of Scadbury Park, or Chislehurst Commons, when he wrote in "The Jew of Malta" the lines:—

> "Where woods and forests go,
> in goodly green
> I'll be Adonis, thou shalt be
> love's queen.
> The meads, the orchards
> and the primrose lanes. "

Did he get his material for "The Massacre at Paris" from the Walsinghams, remembering that Sir Francis was the English ambassador at Paris at that time, with Sir Philip Sidney, who subsequently married Frances Walsingham, taking refuge with him at the Embassy? We do not know, but what we do know is that Marlowe was arrested at Scadbury on the 18th of May, 1593, and taken to Greenwich where he appeared before the Privy Council on a trumped-up charge of heresy.

The charge had been made by a certain Richard Baines, not a very creditable person for he was hanged at Tyburn in the following year for a degrading offence. The Privy Council does not

20

appear to have taken the accusations seriously. No charges were ever proved against him.

They freed him pending further examination, but required him to keep within a few miles of the Court, at Greenwich. This restriction was no doubt irksome for so lively a man and so we are not too surprised to find him, on 30th May, in what must have been a drunken brawl in the house of a certain Eleanor Bull at Deptford Strand. His companions were Ingram Frizer, Robert Poley and Nicholas Skeres, all described by the coroner as gentlemen. They are all known to have been associated with Thomas Walsingham in different spheres and may thus have been companions of Marlowe at Scadbury, which would account for their visiting him in his time of difficulty. There is no accounting for what a man might do in his cups and thus these four, again quoting the coroner's report "could not be at one nor agree about the payment of the sum of pence, that is, le recknynge . . . ". Marlowe drew Frizer's dagger and in the following struggle received a wound above the eye that caused his death.

Thus, at the early age of 29, died Christopher Marlowe, author of seven plays and other lesser works. The manner of his death was kept rather quiet and was not known in detail until 1925 when Dr. Leslie Hotson discovered the Queen's pardon of Ingram Frizer, with the accompanying papers in the Public Record Office. The poet was buried in the churchyard of St. Nicholas, Deptford, on 1st June, 1593, in what is now an unknown grave. A small tablet to his memory, lost in the bombing of the church in world war II, was replaced by a larger one by the Association of Men of Kent and Kentish Men when the building was re-dedicated in 1958.

Altogether, Marlowe's death, attested by a coroner and jury, by the Vicar of Deptford, the Privy Council and the Queen of England, must be one of the best authenticated in all English history, despite which it was brought into question nearly 400 years later.

Marlowe's patron, Thomas Walsingham, was M.P. for Rochester

and was at all times high in the esteem of Queen Elizabeth. His wife, Audrey, was a Lady of Honour to the Queen and to the consort of her successor, James I.

The great Queen, always a little parsimonious, visited Scadbury on July 20/21, 1597, for the obvious purpose, which is revealed in the minutes of the Privy Council, of securing the whole-hearted support of its owner to the raising of Kentish troops against the anticipated second Spanish Armada. The county was not only to raise these troops, but to equip and to pay them as well without any charge upon the State. For his services in this connection, and doubtless for his earlier work on the Continent, Walsingham had his reward. When the Queen arrived at Scadbury, he was plain Thomas Walsingham. When she left on the following day he was Sir Thomas.

In the Chislehurst history published in 1899 we are told that Elizabeth planted a tree "known as Queen Elizabeth's oak, which is still shown in the beautiful avenue leading from St. Paul's Cray Common to the site of the old house." This would appear to be the gaunt, long-dead oak about half way along the drive, although the present lord of the manor, Major John Marsham-Townshend states that since his earliest days he has always known this as "the smugglers' oak."

The fourth Sir Thomas Walsingham died in 1630. Despite attempts to blacken his name, there is no reason to doubt his epitaph in Chislehurst Parish Church, even if, in common with most monumental inscriptions of that period, it is somewhat fulsomely worded. "He was most wise in conducting the affairs of his country, most zealous for peace, most friendly towards his neighbours, most generous to the poor and most famous for a liberal hospitality towards all." He was buried in the vault below the Scadbury Chapel and is commemorated on the second half of the tablet erected to his grandfather, Sir Edmund, in 1581.

The fifth Sir Thomas Walsingham succeeded his father at Scadbury. He was for a number of years Vice-Admiral of Kent and M.P. for Rochester, but was overtaken by the Civil War and, after being arrested by the Parliamentarians, he sold

Scadbury about 1655. The purchaser was Sir Richard Bettenson, whose family held the estate and the two manors for three generations. His granddaughter, Albinia married General William Selwyn, and their granddaughter, another Albinia, married the Hon. Thomas Townshend who thereby succeeded to Scadbury. He it was who pulled down the mediaeval moated house, apparently because it had become unsafe, about the year 1730. In 1752 he bought the mansion of Frognal.

ABOVE: The Walsingham armorial bearings. BELOW: The Hon. Thomas Townshend (1701–1780)

ABOVE: The old archway at Scadbury. BELOW: The Moat Hall, Scadbury.

24

The King posts in the reconstructed Moat Hall (Courtesy of Virginia Stern)

KEMNAL MANOR
AND SIDCUP

Kemnal, the third Chislehurst manor, covered part of what was formerly East Chislehurst, but in more modern times is known only as Sidcup. It is many hundreds of years since this manor had any personal owners. Prior to A.D. 1259 it was held by the Chomenole family (*Ch.* pronounced as *K* in the same way that Kent appears in Domesday Book as *Chent*) but about that year Alexander de Chomenole sold the manor to the Priory of Hornchurch, in Essex. They already owned some land in Chislehurst as confirmed by a charter (1162-1170) of Archibishop Thomas a Becket.

In 1391 the monks sold Kemnal to the famous William of Wykeham ("Manners Makyth Man") Bishop of Winchester, who made it a part of his endowment of New College, Oxford. From that time onwards the manor was leased to a long list of people over the years who were required to provide meat, drink and lodging for the Warden and scholars of the College when they paid their annual visit, and stable room and provender for their horses. They also had to send two faggots, later changed to four horse-loads of charcoal annually.

Few of the many occupants of Kemnal figure with any prominence in local history. Thomas de Sedcopp, who held land of the manor in East Chislehurst, sold it in 1457 to Bernard Cavell who was Constable of the Hundred of Ruxley in which Chislehurst is situated. He had somehow got mixed up in Jack Cade's Rebellion in 1450 and was one of those who received a royal pardon. The affair does not seem to have affected his prosperity.

Bernard Cavell died in 1479. A jury was empanelled and an

inquest held to establish the lands and properties of which the desceased had died possessed. Among the properties was a house 16 acres of land and five acres of woodland called "Sedecoppes", in Chislehurst, held of the wardship of New College as of their Manor of Kemnale. There are many references to Sedcopp (variously spelt) as a surname in old records and also as a place name. Ivette de Settecoppe had her cow stolen as far back as 1317 and there is an even earlier reference in 1254.

The longest single occupancy of the manor house and demesne lands was that of the Comporte family from 1538 to 1776. New College held Kemnal Manor for 480 years until, in 1872, the rising value of land tempted them to sell. The manor was then split up. A small part, with an undistinguished house dating from the last century, retains the old name. The most notable development was the estate of Foxbury on which the late Henry Frederick Tiarks built a fine house, part Jacobean, part French Chateau. His initials, in pierced stone, form the parapet over the porch. Foxbury is now a missionary College.

Sidcup was a long time developing and at the beginning of the XIXth century had a few houses and an inn and was known as Sidcup Street, partly in East Chislehurst and partly in Foots Cray. The boundaries between the two were curiously drawn and produced many anomalies. For example a considerable part of Foots Cray village was in Chislehurst parish. There was an arrangement between the clergy permitting the Foots Cray children to be baptised in Foots Cray church, but in most other matters, particularly on days of national rejoicing, all the school children were brought to the village green at Chislehurst.

It is hard to appreciate that the Chislehurst boundary followed the west side of Rectory Lane, so that Foots Cray church was on the very border. Before the making of Sidcup Hill, this was also the main road to Maidstone! The Black Horse, in Sidcup High Street, was in Foots Cray, but its front door step was in Chislehurst. Sidcup began to grow into a separate community in the middle of the XIXth century. By 1844 it had its own church (St. John the Evangelist) carved out of the old parish of

Chislehurst.

Sidcup Place, within a park now open to the public, was built as a private residence by an officer of engineers in the early part of the XVIIIth century and after passing through several owner-ships became the offices of the Chislehurst & Sidcup Urban District Council in 1934. Sidcup had at last come officially into existence in 1921 when the Foots Cray Council obtained an order changing its name to Sidcup. Since 1965 there have been further changes. On the opposite side of the Green, on the site of Shotts Farm, Charles Minshaw, about the year 1800, built Place Green House, a pleasant Georgian building which, when it came onto the market in 1950, the then Urban District Council wisely preserved as additional Council offices. Minshaw having been lord of the manor of Foots Cray, the house was later as now known as the Manor House.

Thus the name of East Chislehurst gradually disappeared, leaving only one official link: Sidcup Green is still a part of Chislehurst Commons, legally under the jurisdiction of the Board of Conservators of Chislehurst & St. Paul's Cray Commons but, as a matter of convenience, looked after by the new Bexley Borough Council.

Frognal is the oldest and most historic house in East Chisle-hurst. Thomas the Barber was living there in 1253. The Cressells followed and were liberal benefactors of Chislehurst church. Their arms were once portrayed in the lost stained glass of the church windows.

The Dyneleys rebuilt Frognal about 1550 and some small remains of old work, possibly of their time, may still be seen in the cellars. Sir Philip Warwick lived here from the closing years of the Great Rebellion until his death in 1682. His monu-ment in Chislehurst parish church says that "He was an acceptable servant unto King Charles ye 1st in all his extremities and a faithful one to King Charles ye 2nd."

The Tryons came next and also have a memorial in the parish church. It is probable that Frognal was rebuilt in its present form in their time, for a print, dated 1719, shows it much as it is today except that it has lost the five ornamental gables on its main front. It has lost also the magnificent formal ornamental gardens which appear in the picture to stretch away for miles towards two spires standing far apart on the horizon, one of which may be Chislehurst and the other Eltham. Thomas, the last of the Tryons at Frognal, was a worthy man, but an unsuccessful one in business, by reason of which he took his own life in 1747. His estate was thrown into Chancery and was sold in 1752 to the Hon. Thomas Townshend who had married the heiress of Scadbury. His son, also Thomas, served in various Administrations and held the office of Home Secretary which, at that time, included responsibility for the Colonies. He was raised to the peerage as Baron Sydney of Chislehurst in 1783 and became a viscount in 1789. Meanwhile, he was associated with the preparations for the first Australian settlement so that when the first ship, under Captain Arthur Philip, arrived in a certain beautiful bay in New South Wales on 26th January, 1788, they named the place Sydney in his honour. About the same time he was similarly honoured when Sydney, Cape Breton Island, Nova Scotia, was named after him. The motto of the Canadian city is "Droit et Avant" which may also be seen on the Townshend hatchments high up on the walls of the Scadbury Chapel in Chislehurst parish church.

The Sydneys continued at Frognal and were prominent in Chislehurst history for the next hundred years.

ABOVE: Frognal. BELOW: Thomas, 1st Viscount Sidney (1733–1800).

Frognal from a print of 1719.

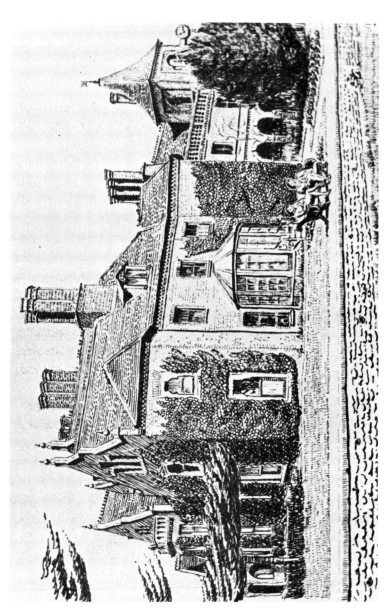

Sidcup Place.

PERISTRETE

"And there is a certain lane or highway leading from Chesilhurst to Fotiscray called Peristrete on the south side of the manor or demesne of Kemynhall". That was written in the year 1530, so Perry Street has a respectable antiquity.

From the Chislehurst end it was originally a direct continuation of Bull Lane (anciently Church Lane), which ran close to the old house of Farringtons towards Foots Cray, but Lord Robert Bertie, towards the end of the XVIIIth century, not liking a public road past his front door, had it diverted round the boundary of his estate, thereby producing a long "S" bend. He built a wall alongside the new road and a great part of it survives nearly 200 years later. In the early 1960's a wide road was made to bypass most of the "S" and what was left was renamed Old Perry Street.

Perry Street is mentioned much before the above date. Richard the Smith held land near Homewood about the year 1250. In 1525 John Warde lived here and called it Piry Streete. In 1527, Joan Cheseman left "a certain grove of wood in Peristrete". She was the daughter and heiress of Bernard Cavell. In 1585, Robert Sissoune lived here and spelled it Peryestrete in Chissilhurst. There can be little doubt that the street took its name from the pear orchards through which it passed.

At the Sidcup end are the thatched cottages of indeterminate date; Frogpool, once Butts Farm, but certainly never a manor as now named. It is a XVIIth century house which, until recently had some fine brick chimneys. Not so long back it had its original long barn with the crookedest roof for many a long mile. No doubt it became too crooked and had to be pulled down. At the junction of old and new Perry Street stood an old smithy known in its later days as Baxter's Forge, just below the Western Motor Works. With the change from the horse to the internal combustion engine the business moved next door. This may well have been the site of the forge of Richard the Smith in the XIIIth century. When the new road came, the old smithy went. It is remembered in the name of Forge House, newly built on the other side of the road. Further on is Cadlands, a house of varying dates going well back, and part weatherboarded.

As we enter Old Perry Street we find houses old and new. We are reminded of days long past on reaching two massive stone gateposts together with the East Lodge of the vanished house of Homewood which was pulled down c. 1920. Its West Lodge, with its twin-shafted porch, is to be seen farther on. Homewood was a large and rather plain Georgian house. Its last owner was Mr. Frank C. Tiarks whose interest was not in the building but in the large estate which stretched back to the borders of his own domain of Foxbury. Here, in the period between the wars, he laid out two polo grounds. The land is now occupied by a Ministry of Defence Depot and by the sports grounds of the Middlesex Hospital, St. Bartholomew's Hospital and the Old Elthamians.

The first house at Homewood was built by a London City Alderman called Cunliffe about 1630. He had unusual arms viz. sable, 3 conies courant or; crest, a greyhound sejant, or collared sable; (three running golden rabbits with black collars and for a crest a seated golden greyhound). The new road runs where the old house once stood.

We now come to the Sydney Arms which was once known as the Swan. For many years the inn sign depicted a pheon, or arrow head, which prompted me to write in 1951 to the Brewery Company asking whether their signwriter had inadvertantly opened the wrong page in a book. A month later the signwriters replied that that had happened and agreeing that the arms displayed were those of the Sidneys of Penshurst. The brewers put this right at the next repainting eleven years later.

On the other side of the road is a banana distribution centre. It has reddish facings and gables, and bears a monogram of two E's (one reversed), with an intertwined letter S, surmounted by an earl's coronet. Until recently a bell hung in one of the gables. This was the school provided by Emily, Countess Sydney, for the children of the Frognal and Scadbury estates and others nearby. On the death of the earl in 1890, the whole of the children, suitably dressed in mourning, lined the road as the funeral cortege went by. Presumably, when the Countess came into full possession of the revenues of the estate she rebuilt her school room, for it bears the date 1891. She died in 1893 and was the last person laid to rest in the burial vault under the Scadbury Chapel in Chislehurst parish church.

Next door to the old school are two old cottages. A third, set right back against a wood, has recently given way to new terrace houses. Similarly, of two old cottages on the other side of the road, one has survived though much restored, and the other, which stood in an ample allotment-type garden, has given way to new houses under the name of Wykeham Court.

Coming towards Chislehurst, we meet. on our left, the old brick wall of Farringtons. Today it is being breached to permit further building. Once a graceful Jacobean house stood here. It had three hipped gables and three sets of tall brick chimneys and was built by Thomas Blencarne (or Blinkhorn), who left his monogram and the date 1649 in the panels of the chimneys. It came into the possession of the Farringtons towards the end of the XVIIth century. The best-known member of the family was General Thomas Farrington who raised a reigment and fought under Marlborough at Ramilles in 1706. He married his neighbour, Theodosia Bettenson of Scadbury, and their daughter Albinia married the first Duke of Ancaster, so that the old house descended to their son Lord Robert Bertie who renamed it Bertie Place. His brother, Captain Lord Thomas Bertie died at Portsmouth and was brought in solemn procession for burial at Chislehurst. His monument in the north aisle of the church displays men-o'-war in action, with the addition of a formidable assortment of the implements of war and flags in basso-relievo. The ducal arms of Ancaster are above. The supporters are, on the right a friar vested in russet with staff and golden rosary; on the left a savage wreathed round the temples and loins. The monument to Lord Robert and his wife adjoins.

On the death of the Berties, the house seems to have reverted to its old name of Farringtons. It went to the Townshends and the last occupant was Miss Mary Townshend who, in accordance with a custom sometimes employed at that time, is described on the Sydney monument in the Scadbury Chapel as "Mrs.". She died in 1821 when the second Viscount Sydney, having no need of the house, pulled it down. He was careful to remove some of the fine Jacobean panelling to Frognal from whence it was later taken to Scadbury. There it may be seen in perfect condition save for a circle of tiny holes where the Home Guard most inconsiderately hung their dart board whilst using the room as Sector Headquarters during World War II.

The site of Farringtons remained undisturbed for ninety years until, on 3rd June, 1910, Sir George H. Chubb (later Lord Hayter) laid the foundation stone of a girls' school. It was opened on 30th June, 1911. The school was enlarged in 1925 when the extension was opened by H.M. Queen Mary on 30th June. A fine chapel was later added. The stables of the old Farringtons had been made into two houses known as Malthouse Cottages, but were pulled down soon after the school was built.

We now emerge at Shepherds Green where stands the fine Prince George Duke of Kent Court, opened as Masonic Homes for the elderly by the present Duke of Kent, in 1968. Shepherds Green was earlier Rands Green after John Rand, Steward to the Farrington family. Rands Farm was nearby on the site of Hollybrake, in Church (now Bull) Lane. The good man left money for the poor widows of Chislehurst. His monument in the parish church says that he lies at the church door, but the door was moved when the building was enlarged in 1849.

Turning southward at Shepherds Green is Holbrook Lane, a

cul-de-sac ending at St. Pauls Cray Common, but surely, in days gone by, going on to join the road to St. Mary Cray that used to run alongside the Scadbury fence? Hoolebrooke Lane is mentioned as far back as 1666, thus sharing with Perry Street the honour of being the oldest-known street names in Chislehurst. The date comes from a lease of the house of Holbrook, the rent of which, at that time, was two barleycorns. The old house (pulled down c. 1960) was almost certainly built by the Poyntells in the XVIIth century. Poyntell Crescent has been built on its paddock or home field, and where pleasant houses now stand, the Chislehurst Volunteers drilled from time to time during World War I.

Judith Poyntell of Holbrook married a Trenchfield. The present Holbrook, built in 1961, consists of commodious modern flats, and rather curiously, in view of its antiquity, all the other houses in Holbrook Lane are of this century.

ABOVE: General Thomas Farrington (1712). BELOW: The old Farringtons.

38

ABOVE: Thos. Farrington, Esq., and nephews: Lords Vere, Montague, Thomas and Robert Bertie. BELOW: Baxter's Forge, c. 1905.

THE CHURCH

Typically Kentish, with walls of flint topped by a shingled broach spire, the old parish church of Chislehurst has preserved much of the beauty and charm of an earlier age.

The earliest record of the church concerns the right of presentation to the living, which was given to the monks of Rochester in A.D. 1089. The Saxon window, discovered in 1957, carries the story back over a thousand years.

The Wills of the more ordinary parishioners give us the dedication of the church as being to St. Nicholas and name the various images before which lights were burned. There were two of St. Mary, one in the middle of the pewless church and another "at the side of the altar". Others mentioned were St. Nicholas, St. Katherine, St. John Baptist, St. James, St. Christopher, St. Anthony and St. Mary Magdalen. This galaxy of twinkling lights disappeared at the Reformation, as did the platform on the screen and the Rood.

Painted on the wall over the arches in the Scadbury Chapel are the royal badges of King Henry 6 and King Edward 4. There are those who ascribe these to William Camden, but as this aisle of the church was built during the Wars of the Roses, and each of the kings concerned reigned twice, it seems more probable that these badges were painted on the orders of the second Thomas Walsingham when enlarging the church. By displaying both badges he would be less likely to offend whichever monarch was on the throne at any time. It should also be noted that Warwick the Kingmaker was lord of the manor and he, as is well known, served both kings as the occasion demanded. The numerals are arabic. These badges were partly restored in 1928.

From old records there emerges the half-told story of William Edelwyne, Edyth his wife, Margery his mother and a mysterious fourth party, Dionysius Bredemongster. This quartette quarrelled in Mottingham in 1278. Whatever the cause, William was so inconsiderate as to cut off his wife's head. There was the usual hue and cry and William fled to Chislehurst parish church, and took sanctuary. To avoid being fined by the king, the villagers surrounded the church to prevent escape and sent for the coroner. The church was paramount in this matter of sanctuary, so that all William had to do was to swear before the coroner that he would flee the country within a specified number of days. This, he doubtless did.

It looks as if there was a new ring of bells, or did they just want repair in 1446 when John Cavyll, father of Bernard, Constable of the Hundred of Ruxley, left 40d. for the purpose? In 1459, Stephen Levendale stated "I Will John and Stephen, my sons, to fence the west side of the graveyard of the parish church of Chysylhurst with pales" and John Thorp was to see that it was done. John Shott, in 1504, left 40s. or more for a cross to be erected in the churchyard: also 13s. 4d. "for the diall of the same church."

The Wills show a great variety of spellings of our place name: Chikishurst (1456); Chysylhurst (1459); Cheselerte (1479); Chesylhurste (1526); Chelesherste (1539) and Chisselhurst (1630).

Although the name of the village priest, curate or minister is often quoted, such names are not found on the list of rectors. This is due to the fact that benefices were held in plurality, the holder appointing a curate (or sometimes none at all) to those parishes from which he took the stipend but in which he did not reside.

The list of recorded Rectors of Chislehurst begins with a local man, Adam de Bromleigh. The date is not given, but is adjudged to have been A.D. 1260. (There were many earlier rectors of whom no records have survived.) John Wilbore, 1523, was a pluralist, for he was also Chaplain to King Henry VIII, Prebendary of Rochester and Master of Newark Hospital at Strood. George Wilson was Rector from 1683 to 1719. The most exciting event in his time was the famous charity sermon on August 14, 1718, preached to obtain alms for the poor children of St. Ann's-within-Aldersgate, some of whom, after marching through the village, were present. Those were the days of the Old Pretender and the licence to preach was granted by Atterbury, Bishop of Rochester.

Perhaps the rumours of Jacobite plots caused the Chislehurst justices to be unduly nervous. They became alarmed at the sight of the ragged children and declared the whole thing seditious. There followed the unseemly scenes in the church when Mr. Thomas Farrington, a son of the General and one of the Justices of the Peace, fought the churchwardens and clergy in the chancel in an attempt to prevent the alms being taken up. He did not succeed, but the preacher, the Rev. Mr. Hendley, and the guardians of the children were arraigned at Maidstone, found guilty of extortion, conspiracy, fraud and sedition, and fined 6s. 8d. each.

The next Rector was Thomas Moore. The mural tablets to him on the south wall of the choir tell us that he rebuilt the Parsonage House. In fact, "T 1735 M" appeared in large black letters and figures under a canopy over the garden door of the rectory until its demolition in 1960.

After him came Francis Wollaston, Rector for 47 years, who died, aged 83, in the year of Waterloo.

He had a considerable reputation as an author of theological and other works and as an astronomer. He it was who entertained the whole of his parishioners, 2,000 of them, on the village green after the signing of the Treaty of Paris in 1814. If these are not sufficient claims to fame, he had 17 children, one of whom painted a number of surviving pictures. The late Sir Gerald Woods Wollaston, sometime Garter King of Arms, was a descendant and often came to Chislehurst.

This was the great preaching era and, as the churches were

poorly heated, the Georgians introduced their own standards of comfort. The wealthier families erected boxes, provided their own chairs and cushions, and sometimes a fireplace as well, complete with a chimney rising up through the roof. These were the typical box pews of the period. Miss Wollaston's painting, made about 170 years ago, gives us a good idea of what they were like at Chislehurst. There were two galleries against the west wall; one for the tenants of the manor and another, just under the ceiling, for the singers and musicians.

There was no chancel arch. The rood screen had "The lion roreth. His strength is as an unicorn" painted upon it, presumably in reference to the royal arms of King Charles II which had once stood in the centre, but which seem later to have been moved to a position above the altar on the east wall. In 1786 a clock was placed in the church tower at the cost and charge of Richard Barwell, the owner of Homewood, on condition that he be allowed to divert a footpath within his grounds leading into Perry Street. The new path was thereafter called Clock Alley and provided a circular walk via Belmont Lane by Kemnal Manor to Perry Street and Ashfield Lane. In 1925, when the Grammar School for Girls was built in Beaverwood Road, it was thought undesirable to have a footpath nearby and family Sunday walks having by then begun to go out of fashion, Clock Alley was closed.

The next incumbent was Francis Dawson, a pluralist who was for many years non-resident. He allowed his curate to live in the Rectory, but, to bring in a little more money, let the whole of the gardens as a potato field.

The next Rector of Chislehurst (in 1846) was Francis Henry Murray, son and grandson of a bishop. He found the church in a parlous condition, with services held on Sundays only and Holy Communion celebrated six times per annum. He immediately cleared the old box pews, added a south aisle and porch, rebuilt most of the chancel and erected a chancel arch, bringing the building substantially as we see it today. The pews he fitted still remain, together, in many cases, with additional draw-out seats for use when the church is full. All the pews at one time had doors. The church was re-consecrated by Archibishop John Sumner on 23rd October, 1849, which day is kept each year as the Dedication Festival.

RECTORS OF CHISLEHURST

(The names of the Rectors prior to A.D. 1260 are not on record)

1260 ADAM DE BROMLEIGH
1267 WILLIAM
1308 WALTER DE BEDEWINDE
1310 RICHARD DE LONDON
1315 STEPHEN
1316 JOHN DE WILMINGTONE
1334 WILLIAM DE HONYNGTON
1336 EDMUND DYGGE
1337 WILLIAM DE ESTWELLE
1339 THOMAS DE ALKHAM
1346 RICHARD DE SCHOLDONE
1348 WILLIAM DE WALMERE
1361 JOHN VERIEU
1361 ROBERT CARY, S.T.P.
1362 RICHARD DE UTTOXETRE
1372 JOHN HAMONDE
1412 WILLIAM GELOT
1421 JOHN TRAFFORD
1426 ADAM DE RACETON
1438 JOHN RAGOLF
1443 RICHARD MANNYNG
1446 THOMAS FEYSEY
1446 ALAN PORTER
1482 JOHN WOODROFFE, S.T.P.
1508 WILLIAM TOFTE
1509 GEORGE OR GEOFFREY DEKAR
1515 EDWARD HYGGINS
1518 GEORGE DAWNER

1520 RICHARD SHARPE, S.T.B.
1523 JOHN WILBORE, LL.B.
    Chaplain to King Henry VIII.
    Prebendary of Rochester.
1552 ROBERT GARRET
1567 THOMAS DILWORTH
1571 JAMES SAYER
1579 SAMUEL ATHERTON, A.B.
1583 THOMAS KENDALL
1586 RICHARD HARVEY, M.A.
1630 RICHARD CHASE, M.A.
1647 WILLIAM HUSSEY
1653 RICHARD EDWARDS
1669 DAVID BARTON, M.A.
1683 GEORGE WILSON, M.A.
1719 THOMAS MOORE, S.T.P.
1769 FRANCIS WOLLASTON, LL.B.
1815 FRANCIS DAWSON, M.A.
1846 FRANCIS HENRY MURRAY,
    M.A. *Hon. Canon of Canterbury*
1902 JAMES EDWARD DAWSON, M.A.
    Hon. Canon of Rochester
1930 OSCAR HARDMAN, D.D.
1936 JOHN REGINALD LUMB, M.A.
    Canon Emeritus of Blackburn
1955 REGINALD GEORGE II.
    McCAHEARTY, M.A.
    Archdeacon of Bromley
1967 STEPHEN HOWARD ADAMS, M.A.

ABOVE: The Parish Church, 1789. BELOW: In 1871.

Orate pro aia Alani Porter quondam dñi Rectoris istius
ecclesie qui obijt die mensis Maii A°dñi
M°CCCC°lxxxij° cuius Anime propiciet ds Amen

ABOVE: Alan Porter d.1482. BELOW: The Parish Church; early 19th century painting.

ABOVE: Francis Wollaston, Rector 1769–1815. BELOW: Inside the Church; early 19th century painting.

ABOVE: The Church in 1857. BELOW LEFT: Badge of Edward IV in the Parish Church; BELOW RIGHT: Badge of Henry VI in the church.

48

COCKPIT AND GREEN

Despite an increasing population, the village green of Chislehurst remains unspoilt and will probably remain so as long as the Commons Conservators resist the temptation to put their motor mowers on it. Unlike many other village greens in Kent, it is not required for cricket, for which there is provision elsewhere. There is a quite remarkable variety of grasses. In one particular spot a "fairy ring" of hare-bells appears each year, and from the site of the 1953 coronation bonfire, the parish church may be viewed, in summer, over a galaxy of rosebay willow herb.

A lithograph of 1858 shows the green devoid of trees and it is hard to believe that the oaks now there, compared with that planted within the village pound in 1911, can be no more than a hundred years old. Gorse adds a touch of gold, as does a laburnum, in due season.

In the centre is the cockpit, claimed to be the most perfect of its kind in all England. It is in line with the east-west axis of the church, and retains its bowl complete, together with a slightly raised inner ring for the supervising of events. Cockfighting was abolished by Act of Parliament in 1834. At the annual fairs held here, the cockpit was used for single-stick and other contests and these, it seems, continued for some time after the fair, having become a nuisance, was abolished in 1862.

This part of the green was for long the established place of assembly for the villagers on great national occasions.

Until the 1930's, the village green also attracted coconut shies and stalls on the Whitsun and August Bank Holidays each year.

Many of the houses in Church Row are Georgian, of the

1830's, or thereabouts, built of Chislehurst bricks and with Chislehurst chimney pots bearing the name of Pascall of the White Horse brickfields. Beyond these Georgian residences, as one nears the War Memorial, are three interesting survivials intact at present, but quite likely to be gone before long. These old houses were attached to a brewery that flourished behind what is now the chemists' shop on the Royal Parade at the end of the XVIIIth century. The largest of the three houses was built for the master brewer and the two smaller ones for the workers.

Behind the back gardens of these houses was a row of stables that survived until a few years ago when they became unsafe and had to be taken down, saving the waggoner's cottage at the end. The last stall at the end of the stables was reserved for any horse that might be sick, and it was the waggoner's duty to come down in the middle of the night should he hear his charges coughing or otherwise restive. The cottage is tiny indeed, with one room up and one down. In the lower room the original firegrate remains. Round the walls are huge harness pegs. Whether these survive from the days of the brewery, or from the time when Mr. A. Travers Hawes stabled his carriage and horses here at the beginning of this century is not known.

Despite this being the highest part of Chislehurst, each of these houses in Church Row once had a deep well and it was from these that the water came to save the church during the fire in 1857. All are now closed, but one or two pumps remain, producing water that is cold and hard.

"Franks of the Brewhouse" appears in the accounts of the Blackneys, blacksmiths, in 1800. At some time after that the brewery closed and the land between the two roads (not yet named Royal Parade and Church Row) became a farm with the largest house as the farmhouse and the others as the homes of the labourers.

Next door is Jasmine Cottage and next again an old house which was long known as "Teatime" and much favoured for the atmosphere of its parlour. It no longer serves teas and it shares its front with an antique shop. Much earlier this century this was Chislehurst's main post office. Next is a house, probably early Victorian, that served as council offices when Chislehurst had its own Urban District Council.

In our perambulation of the village green we now turn left into the appropriately named School Road to face, on the commons, St. Michael's Orphanage, a group of buildings that include the old Poor House built in 1759. The treatment of the poor and aged two hundred years ago left much to be desired, but Chislehurst people seem to have done something to mitigate the harshness of the times. To build this place they consolidated a number of local charities and obtained an Act of Parliament for the purpose. From time to time the local gentry got together to subsidize the cost of bread. In 1800 a soup kitchen was opened and soup was sold at one penny per quart.

On the other side of the picture, one of the overseers reported to the Vestry in 1808 that the allowance for one day's subsistence in the Poorhouse was one herring and three potatoes per person and that, in consequence, he found that the inmates were starving. The Vestry appointed a butcher, but finding that he supplied more bones than meat, they changed in favour of Mr. Gravett whose shop was in one of the old cottages adjacent to Walton Lodge that still bears his name. In due time, the care of the poor became a national responsibility and after the opening of the Bromley Union Workhouse at Farnborough, the local one was closed. From 1834 to 1836 it became a girls' school and the pupils were taught to make their own uniforms consisting of a waistless bright green serge frock, a check bibbed apron and a white mob cap. The old Poor House was then divided into tenements and so remained until it was bought by the trustees of St. Michael's Orphanage in 1855.

Next are the St. Nicholas Church of England Schools (long known as the National Schools) which with "The Crown" and other buildings, occupy an island site marked on old maps as

51

"the Bowling Alley" of the nearby mansion of the Bowles family (now Camden Close). This land had been taken from the commons as is clearly shown in a lease dated 1st May, 1712, granted by Sir Edward Bettenson, Baronet, to William Harris, Yeoman, of two acres "heretofore inclosed out of a Comon called Chisselhurst Comon or Chisselhurst Heath." The rent was "two fat pulletts or four shillings at the Feast of the Nativity of Our Saviour."

It was one of Sir Edward Bettenson's successors as lord of the manor, Lord Sydney, who gave the north end of this island site to the parish in 1836 for the building of a school for boys and girls. There had been one or two charity schools previously, but with a small intake. The National School was first enlarged in 1867 when the first building became the master's house and so served until, just over a hundred years later it has been taken into the school buildings again. There were further additions in 1874 and the quadrangle was completed in 1908. The headmaster then was Mr. F.R. Greenfield, affectionately known to most of the parish as "Tubby". He was Clerk to the Board of Conservators and with their consent he had drainage trenches dug in the old gravel pit alongside the school and set the boys the laborious task of picking up all the loose stones with which to fill them. The parents subscribed a sum sufficient for levelling, the floor of the pit was seeded with grass, and thus the school secured its present playground.

This group of mellowed red brick buildings, standing directly on the commons and facing the village green, forms a pleasing feature. The interior has been modernised, but because of the age of the buildings and the lack of an enclosed playground, the school does not comply with the Education Act of 1944 and is threatened with closure. There are proposals for a new building on the glebe in Bull Lane.

"The Crown" was built in 1874, moving there from its former site in Crown Lane. "The White House" is the oldest building on this island site and part, if much renewed, survives from the "old decayed house" mentioned in William Harris's lease of

1712.

Crossing Watts Lane and passing, for the moment, Bishopswell, we enter Morley Road along the garden wall of "Ivy House". Here lived John Nussey, Apothecary and Physician-in-Ordinary to three successive monarchs. He attended King George IV on his deathbed at Windsor in June, 1830, which he described in a letter to his wife as having left him completely exhausted. Adding, in a lighter tone "I have got for you the very handkerchief in use when he died." He came into possession also of the nightcap worn by the king on his deathbed, a strange affair of stockinet at least six feet long; also the bedspread of pink, yellow, green and purple, and two tiny shirts made for Princess Charlotte's stillborn baby.

Apothecary John Nussey was in due time called upon to prepare the oil for the coronation of Queen Victoria on 31st June, 1838, and the queen's wishes were conveyed to him that she would dislike both musk and jessamine and would prefer the mildest kinds of perfume, which document, together with others, his court dress and sword, the mementoes mentioned above and a cup presented to him by the Society of Apothecaries in 1834 remained in the Nussey family for over a century.

John Nussey ran his practice from a house in Cleveland Row, St. James' from which he attended on the Royal household. He seems first to have leased Ivy House as a country residence in 1843. He died in 1862. His son, Antony Foxcroft Nussey, lived for a time at Richmond, but came back to resume the lease of the Ivy House, which he eventually bought. He was for twenty years a churchwarden here. Miss Helen, the last of the "Ivy House" Nusseys, spent her last years at "The White House" across the way. The relics of King George IV went to the Brighton Pavilion Museum and the letters and similar items to the Society of Apothecaries in London.

For many years, the Ivy House was notable for a massive arched entrance of clipped yew. The house was unoccupied on 27th July, 1944, when a V.I. flying bomb fell in Crown Lane and rendered it completely uninhabitable. Restoration reduced it from three storeys to two. The yew arch has gone; so has the old cottage at the northern end.

Next door, until 1944, stood two semi-detached weatherboarded cottages, built about the year 1800. Rosemary Cottage was long tenanted by the Mitcham family who displayed a large sign "Tea Rooms" and erected a small marquee in the front garden every Spring.

No vestige of these cottages remains. They were first damaged one evening towards the end of the Battle of Britain in the late summer of 1940 when a stick of bombs fell at Scadbury, Manor Park Road, Rectory Place and the last on the village green by Morley Road. A difference in the grasses still indicates the site of the last to fall. The damage was repaired, but the cottages were not so fortunate on 27th July, 1944, when a flying bomb, already mentioned, fell in Crown Lane. Jessamine Cottage, "opened up like a packing case, and the whole external wall facing Ivy House was pulled right away from the structure several feet."

We now come to Norman Cottage, probably built by one Thomas Field, builder and carpenter, towards the end of the XVIIIth century. He left it to his nephew, Edward Whight, who carried on the same business and in whose family it remained for three generations. He it was who built the two cottages just described. A grandson, Thomas Whight, got into debt and in 1856, by Order of the Queen's Bench, the whole of the contents of the house had to be sold. In this four-bedroomed house there were, surprisingly, twelve bedsteads, four of them four-posters and eight of the more ordinary kind, together with rosewood chairs, mahogany sideboards and much else. They fetched a total of £45 2s. 0d. as certified by Richard Paterson, Sheriff, of an inventory. Happily, the man who had foreclosed had a heart, for he left the Whights in possession of their furniture so long as they lived, by executing a deed appointing Mrs. Whight as his agent "in charge of the goods".

A mortgage deed of 1857 quotes the same Thomas Whight as a Carpenter and Retailer of Beer, which seems to confirm a local tradition that Norman Cottage was once an alehouse known as "The Union Jack". It certainly has an adequate cellar. It later came into the ownership of Captain Bowden, of Coopers, who gave it its present name after that of his first wife who came of the Norman family of Bromley Common. He established a small orphanage for boys here, and built a Roman Catholic school (now St. Mary Hall) on the rear part of the estate in Crown Lane. There have been a number of subsequent owners.

The southern part of Morley Road was developed by Charles Morley, of Coopers, towards the end of the last century.

Entering Hawkwood Lane, we face the old garden wall of Coopers which, together with the trees planted on the green by the Conservators in recent times, do their best to hide the modern extensions to Coopers School. Built within the eastern end of the Coopers property are the Sydney Homes for Old People, opened in September 1965. On the site, and unused, one supposes, for the past century or more, was a relic of the seventeen hundreds in the form of a large, deep ice-house, its dome covered with mature trees and scrub. Efforts were made to preserve it, but the ground was needed and it had to go.

The old, weatherboarded houses known as Rectory Place are less in number than they used to be, for, on that same summer evening during the Battle of Britain, a bomb fell on No. 1, demolishing it entirely. The occupant, Mr. Heggety, was taking a bath at the time, but the bath took him and he suddenly found himself, still seated in it, in his front garden! He suffered only scratches. A row of small cottages near the old fire station were so damaged that they had to be demolished.

We emerge now facing the lychgate, having passed an island of buildings that include "The Tiger's Head", an old-established hostelry of obvious antiquity as it clearly derives its name from the tiger crest of the Walsinghams who left Chislehurst in or about 1655. Its proprietor undertook the catering for Rector Wollaston's feast on the green in 1814, and again on 19th April, 1822, for the inaugural dinner of the West Kent Cricket Club after its transfer to Chislehurst from Princes Plain on Bromley

Common.

In Church Lane we see the Village Hall, basically the same as when built in 1867 despite its appearance. The Annexe was built at the cost and charge of the late Sophie Louise Tiarks very early in the present century. In it she ran a boys' club almost unaided for a quarter century or more.

"The Bull's Head", so far as its name is concerned, reminds us of one of the crests of Warwick the Kingmaker, lord of the manor of Chislehurst in the XVth century. It may date from that period, but the first mention we find of it is on a map dated 1680. There is nothing in the present building earlier than the Adam Room, with a fine XVIIIth century ceiling. John Turner was the landlord here in 1792 and was perhaps famous for his roasts, for in that year he paid Blackney the Smith "for clanen a rosten jack", and, later, "for setten the old jack to rights". Perhaps there were highwaymen about in 1800 when Turner got the smith to clean his pistol and lock. After paying one shilling for a new well handle, he disappears from the Blackney accounts. The building was lengthened at the north end towards the end of the XIXth century.

Opposite "The Bull's Head" at the entrance to Bull Lane is "Abury", a house that may well have witnessed the passing cavalcade of the first Elizabeth on her way to and from Scadbury in 1597. From old estate maps we find that the cottage and adjoining baker's shop once belonged to General Farrington, whose son, in 1754, leased them to William Phillips. In 1824, the property was described as a house, bakehouse, buildings and gardens of two rods and two perches leased to George Gimson. The place was known as Gimson's Farm, but was also the village bakery.

In the 1850's the baker was William Barham, which I might not have known had I not married his great-granddaughter. When Sarah Ann Barham married James Nicholls, her father made over the old house to them and here the young couple (they were married in the parish church on Christmas Day, 1866) ran a market garden.

Towards the end of the XIXth century, St. George's Hall, a timber structure of unusual plan, was built on the north side of the garden of "Abury", for or by the Primrose League. Its vestibule to Bull Lane was long and narrow—perhaps four or five times longer than the hall itself. On 16th October, 1940 it fell a victim to a German bomb that also seriously damaged the house.

Across the way, in Bull Lane, stand Mr. J.H. Easden's premises (formerly St. Nicholas Mens' Club) and at the rear of these premises one of the last German V.2. rockets fell on 13th March, 1945, setting fire to that building and destroying most of the furniture stored there by people who had lost their homes by the bombing. The explosion brought down more plaster and ceilings at "Abury", revealing massive timbers underneath, not previously exposed.

Royal Parade, strictly speaking, is confined to the other side of the road. It was given its name soon after the arrival of the Imperial family of France in 1870, but Walton Lodge and the nearby cottages are of much older date. The cellar of Walton Lodge is said to contain a spring and in the days when the church organ was pumped by water power, the occupants of this house were always able (so it is said) to know when the sermon had ended, by going down into their cellar. A similar story was told some years ago by Keeper Cox in respect of the stream on the common running into the Rush Pond. Furthermore, when the church changed to electric power, the ponds dried up!

An old water colour, attributed to a daughter of Rector Wollaston, c.1814 shows "the elegant feast on Chislehurst Common . . . 7th July, 1814."

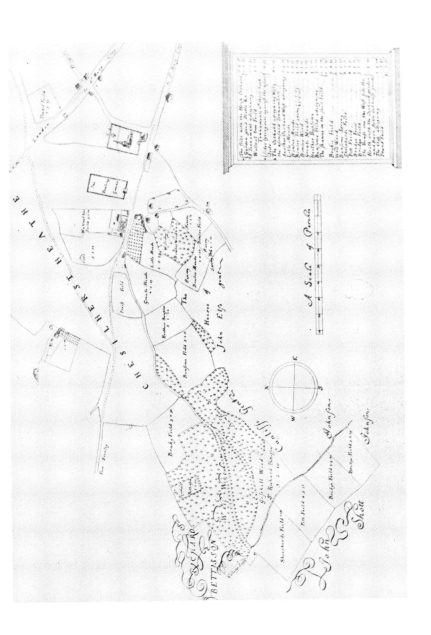

A plan of part of Chislehurst c.1680.

ABOVE: William Barham, baker of Royal Parade, 1860 (Courtesy the Misses M. & B. Pott) BELOW: The old cottages by the church, demolished in 1894.

ABOVE: The Green in 1868. BELOW: The Village Hall, 1868.

ABOVE: United Service at the Cockpit, for George V's Silver Jubilee, May 6, 1935. BELOW: Rosemary and Jessamine Cottages, c. 1880.

OLD ROADS & VANISHED PLACES

To accommodate horse-drawn traffic there were a number of tracks across the Commons which have long since disappeared. One skirted the perimeter of Prickend Pond between Green Lane and the High Street. Another ran direct from "The Crown" to "The Tiger's Head". A third skirted the Overflow pond from Bromley Road to the Station Road.

The Overflow really did overflow in those days, but, due to changes in the weather, or a drop in the water table, it rarely does today. Up to recent times there was a small pond by the roadside near "The Briars" (now "Briars Place") and up to 1899 there was the horse pond of Red Hill Farm where now stand the International, Co-operative and other shops in the High Street.

Webster's pond was something of a favourite. It was on the Commons at the junction of Ashfield Lane and Kemnal Road, facing the house known as "Woodlands", long the residence of the Webster family, which was demolished to make way for the modern Roehampton Drive. The pond was parallel to the road so that traps could be driven through it to clean the wheels and freshen the horses. The Conservators long ago filled in Websters Pond.

The best known of the lost roads of Chislehurst was the one which continued from Heathfield Lane through the common to St. Nicholas' School. It was closed between the wars to avoid the crossings that it entailed of Centre Common Road and Bromley Road. None of these roads received their present names until about 1948.

Under this lost road is the water course that drains the

Overflow, and, on its way to the Rush pond goes under the wide path on the east side of the main road. This was once the starting point of a racecourse. The horses did a "U" turn above Prickend Pond and then ran south on the other side of the main road, both of these courses being free of trees and undergrowth up to fifty years ago. The crossing of Bromley Road was marked by two whalebone posts and the finish at the gates of Camden Court by two more. There is also said to have been a whalebone arch at one time within the grounds, placed there by Admiral Wells or another member of that family. Camden Court, whose last residents were the Bilbroughs, was demolished between the wars and the extensive grounds filled by Camden Close.

Continuing, we enter Crown Lane by the modern house of "Bishopswell" replacing that lost by enemy action in 1944. The old house had in its grounds a well said to have been blessed by the Bishops of Rochester when they lived in Bromley Palace in the days of long ago. Here, among others, lived Mr. G.B. Wollaston, a collector of rare trees and a friend of the Empress Eugenie. Next door was a creeper-covered weatherboarded old house then known as "Well Cottage", and next to that the one-time "Crown Inn", then called "Old Crown Cottage" and now "Crown House".

On 27th July, 1944 a V.1. flying bomb fell in front of "Well Cottage", reducing it and "Old Crown Cottage" to a heap of ruins but, the last named was a timber-framed building of considerable antiquity and the owner, Miss Thornton, was saved by a staunch upright timber which held up the surrounding wreckage. The old inn once had small, leaded panes, some bearing the initials of habitues of earlier days, the floor was two feet below ground level, and as was to be expected in a building linked with the days of smuggling, there was a large cellar. A map of 1712 shows the end of the garden of what is now "Ivy House" across the road as "Garden of the Rose and Crown". Some of the old timbers were incorporated in the rebuilding that is now "Crown House".

The narrow Crown Lane has a number of Victorian and

Edwardian villas and, at its upper end, "Barn End", once a barn, then an evangelical meeting place, now a dwelling. Here is St. Mary's Roman Catholic Church, built by the Bowden family in 1854. "Coopers", in Hawkwood Lane, took its name from the man who built it in the XVIIIth century, Francis Cooper. He was succeeded by Sir Richard Adams, a judge, whose monument in the church says that he died of the gaol fever "caught in the Old Bayly" in 1774. The Bowdens followed. Lord Richard Cavendish later lived here, as did Charles Morley.

For some years in this century, this was a private girls' school under the name of Tudor Hall, but after World War II it was acquired by the Kent County Council and, with the addition of modern extensions, became Coopers School. A separate school for handicapped children has recently been built within the campus.

At the end of the metalled road, until 1960, stood the old "Hawkwood" with a curious agglomeration of styles, Georgian and Victorian; with 50 to 60 rooms and a somewhat fantastic skyline of saddleback tower, gables, chimneys (some concealed in a turret) and a bellcote. At one time Mann's Farm, later Goodlands and finally Hawkwood, it had a history going back to the XVIth century. Until 1960, it had an unaltered Georgian laundry and drying room, with a large iron boiler encased in wood, together with contemporary bins. On the wall was a leaden plate bearing the date 1796 and, over the pump, another marked "RJ 1804" for Robert Jenner, the owner at that time. In the drying room was a mangle reputedly 200 years old and weighing nearly a ton. In 1961 it was given by Mrs. R. Hall to the Oxhey Wood House Museum of Wooden Bygones at Northwood, Middlesex, together with some contemporary gear.

The old Hawkwood was occupied for nearly a hundred years by the Edlmann family. The late Col. F.J.F. Edlmann, D.S.O., was, in 1919, the founder President of the Chislehurst Branch of the National Federation of Discharged and Demobilised Sailors and Airmen (which later merged in the British Legion). The Colonel served Chislehurst in many other ways, not least in the purchase of the remaining part of Petts Wood to keep it from speculative builders. Two other benefactors in the persons of Mr. & Mrs. Robert Hall purchased the entire Hawkwood estate and in 1958 gave the greater part of it to the National Trust, reserving only the immediate environs of the house for their own use.

The great rambling house, which had gone unrepaired for decades, had to be pulled down. Two smaller dwellings have been built in its place. In the garden is a magnificent avenue of limes continuing the line of Hawkwood Lane which once ran on past the front of the house. The public only had pedestrian rights and these were diverted down Botany Bay Lane into a path which ran down to the Kyd Brook and Gosshill Road. Because this was tightly enclosed within iron, fencing, it was known as Birdcage Walk. The path remains, free and open under the National Trust.

From Watts Lane, another lost road ran alongside "The Briars" and, skirting the cricket ground, ran down the hill to Gosshill Road. A house there, standing end on, shows where it emerged. This road was closed when Summer Hill was opened to the public in 1865. Here stood the Water Tower, built by Mr. George Wythes as the front gate to his Bickley Estate (although the actual gates were never fitted). On it he placed his arms in stone and one of the panels has been preserved with the intention of incorporating it into a seat to mark the site of the tower on top of the hill. Here also, from 1796 until 1876 stood a fine windmill, originally built by ten local people, including the lord of the manor and the rector, partly on common land, with special facilities for grinding for the poor. The ten were gradually bought out, one by one, until Mr. G.H. Baskcomb, making the final take-over, obtained a team of horses, attached ropes to the cap of the mill, and down it all came. His efforts to enclose and sell the common land were frustrated by the commoners who pulled down his fences as fast as he erected them. Canon Murray championed the cause of his parishioners and presided at a crowded meeting which unanimously agreed to take such steps in law as were open to it. The common land was restored.

The mill had its own little road across the cricket ground, long since grassed over. Chislehurst Cricket Ground is one of the few in England which enjoys that status by Act of Parliament, the West Kent Cricket Club, which moved here from Princes Plain in 1822, having statutory rights to play there.

The last of our lost roads began near the entrance to Scadbury where the roads to Orpington and to St. Mary Cray originally divided. The latter ran along the Scadbury fence, opposite which, at one time, were two weatherboarded cottages on an island site on St. Paul's Cray Common. These were built as a smithy by the first Lord Sydney at the end of the XVIIIth century and were first occupied by the Blackneys. When Leesons Hill was carried up to the Orpington Road in the mid XIXth century, the old road was closed and these houses, as it were found themselves back to front. They were then occupied by the Dabner family who continued the bakery here with wood fires in the ovens.

Dabners Cottages were destroyed by fire on 22nd May, 1937, and to find their site one should look for an apple tree amidst the nettles and ferns, taking care to avoid the well. The old road went on across the modern Leesons Hill to the "Robin Hood" Inn which still survives as two dwellings and which had remains many years ago of the bars, bottle-glass windows and the inn cellar together with the ancient stabling, long since gone.

ABOVE: An early 19th century view of Chislehurst Mill. BELOW: The Old
Bishopswell c.1910.

ABOVE: The Water Tower, 1871. BELOW: Hawkwood, 1899.

Dabners' Cottages, destroyed in 1938.

ABOVE: Charles Dabner, (1852–1931). BELOW: The Mill, 1860. (Courtesy of F. Pierce).

IMPERIAL CHISLEHURST

Time was when the tricolour of France could be seen above the trees on Chislehurst Common; when an Emperor and an Empress trod its shady walks and the village gained its epithet "Imperial".

Camden Place, residence of the Imperial Family of France during the 1870's, stands on the site of the house of "the great and learned William Camden, one of the most erudite writers, industrious antiquaries and˙faithful historians, England has to boast"—so wrote Virtue in his "Picturesque Beauties of Great Britain" in or about the year 1830. Camden was Headmaster of Westminster School, Clarenceux King of Arms, and author of "Britannia", the first topographical description of England. He lived here from 1609 to 1623 and in his Will directed that he should be buried "in that place where it shall please God to call me to His Mercye", but although he died in Chislehurst his wishes were overborne and he was buried in Westminster Abbey in the Poets' Corner. He left £8 to the poor of Chislehurst and £7 to Mr. Richard Harvie, the Rector at that time. In the frieze of the drawing room of the present house is a painting of a long, rather low building, said to represent the house in Camden's time. He is remembered in several of our street names, among them Camden Close, Camden Grove, Camden Park Road and Lower Camden.

Later in the XVIIth century the house was occupied by a branch of the old Chislehurst family of Ellis. Robert Weston bought it in the early 1700's and rebuilt it in unpretentious fashion, enclosing a strip of land from the common on which he planted the double avenue of trees the eastern line of which, within the fence, is still technically a part of Chislehurst Common.

It was Weston who first used the name of Camden Place.

After passing through the hands of two other owners, Camden Place was bought by Charles Pratt, a noted advocate who later became Lord Chancellor of England and became Lord Camden. About the year 1700 he built the centre part of the present house, leaving Weston's earlier building to serve as the domestic portion. He also introduced the fine Jacobean panelling in the entrance hall.

In 1805 Camden Place was purchased by Mr. Thomson Bonar who, with his wife, was foully murdered by a man-servant in the early hours of 31st May, 1813. The assassin was publicly hanged on Penenden Heath, near Maidstone. The tall rectangular stone tomb of the Bonars is to be found close to the lych gate of the parish church. Thomson Bonar, son of the unfortunate couple, continued to live in the house for a time, but the associations were too strong and the place was then left successively to Count Mirfelt, Prince Esterhazy and Count Lieven. They were followed by the Martins, who were bankers, and then by the Rowles who also had a house in Mayfair. It is at this point that the Napoleonic connection begins.

Henry Rowles was Chairman of the Globe Insurance and the builder of Drury Lane Theatre. His wife, who was of Spanish descent, was a noted beauty, as was their youngest daughter, Emily. She was baptised in Chislehurst parish church on 29th October, 1823, and so was probably sixteen or seventeen years of age when, possibly during the London season, the eyes of a certain exiled prince fell upon her. He was Louis Napoleon, son of Louis Bonaparte.

The Bonapartes were exiled from France after the Battle of Waterloo, but this did not prevent the young Louis, although the third son, from forming an ambition to secure the throne of France, an ambition which he eventually achieved in a series of events strangely linked with the story of Chislehurst.

Prince Louis' attraction to Emily Rowles is said to have been at all times an honourable one. In the late 1830's he was a frequent visitor to Camden Place and, following the death of his grandmother, the Empress Josephine, he is said to have offered Emily her furs and other gifts in anticipation, it seemed, of an engagement. But all the time political ambitions were uppermost in his mind. He had already staged an ineffective coup d'etat at Strasbourg and now, in 1840, he embarked on that curious expedition to Boulogne in a paddle steamer with a tame eagle secured to the mast, hoping that on landing the local populace would raise the cry of "Vive Napoleon". Instead they promptly arrested him and sent him to Paris where King Louis Philippe's Court of Peers sentenced him to perpetual imprisonment in the Castle of Ham on the Somme.

At this time, for reasons unknown, Henry Rowles took his own life in his Mayfair house, his widow re-married and the family left Camden Place for Florence, from which place, according to some accounts, Emily sent her prince "prisoner-of-war" parcels, eventually, in 1846, facilitating his escape by sending the workman's clothing that permitted him to walk out of the castle, take a carriage to a railway station and cross the frontier into Belgium. After this, Emily Rowles disappears from the scene for a number of years and one can only wonder whether the discovery that her prince had fathered two sons in the castle of Ham may have made a difference. That she maintained contact with him over that period is not fully substantiated.

Prince Louis Napoleon was soon back in London where he turned his attention to Elizabeth Howard (or Haryett) of equal beauty to the Chislehurst girl, but undoubtedly more sophisticated, having borne a son to a major of the Guards who, as a good old English gentleman, in return settled upon her certain estates in Piccadilly that soon brought in huge sums. These were not vested in the lady, but in a trustee, and that trustee was Nathaniel William Strode who was later to become the owner of Camden Place.

There is no doubt that Elizabeth was devoted to him and that she applied her money in the furtherance of his political ambitions so that, on the fall of Louis Philippe in 1848, Louis Napoleon was able to secure election to the Constituent Assembly of the Second French Republic, become its President at the end of the same year and, in 1852, eventually make himself Emperor of the French.

As Emperor, Napoleon III had to seek a legal wife whom he found in the person of another noted beauty, Maria Eugenia Guzman y Palafox y Porto Carrero, Countess of Teba and Mora, Duchess of Penaranda, second daughter of the Count of Montijo of Spain. They were married in Notre Dame, in Paris, on 29th January, 1853, the bride being then 26 years of age. Miss Howard retired to the Chateau de Beauregard on the outskirts of Paris, where she set up house for herself, her son by Major Martin of the Guards and the Emperor's two sons by Mlle. Vergeot, born in the Castle of Ham. It was thought proper that she should be made "respectable" and so she went through a nominal marriage ceremony with Clarence Trelawney at St. James', Piccadilly, London, at which the principal witness was Nathaniel William Strode of Chislehurst. Mrs. Trelawney died in 1865 and was buried in a cemetery near her chateau.

N.W. Strode bought Camden Place in 1860 and immediately began the task of transforming it into a minor French chateau. Two protruding wings were added, the dimensions of which were determined by some XVIIIth century panelling from the Chateau de Bercy which he had bought and wished to use unaltered. It graces the dining room to this day, with the original doors and hinges exactly as they were in the hunting box of the Bourbon kings of France. Strode also bought the fine wrought iron gates of the Paris Exposition of 1867 and they remained at the entrance to Camden Place, their lamps topped with golden crowns, until they were senselessly smashed in the summer of 1940, ostensibly to furnish scrap iron for the war effort. Strode also went to great lengths to obtain French furnishings and fittings for the interior of the house and erected a well-head in the park said to be an exact copy of a similar one at St. Cloud. The Emperor, during his exile, is said to have regarded this as "a touch of home."

It was claimed at the time that all this work at Camden Place was undertaken by Mr. Strode under a premonition that Napoleon III would some day need a refuge in England, but, after the fall of the Second Empire, the French state papers revealed that he had been paid Fcs. 900,000.00 from the Emperor's civil list. Whether this was in repayment of Miss Howard's loans for the advancement of his cause as emperor will never be known. It is most unlikely that the Empress had any knowledge of these proceedings.

Things were getting difficult for the Emperor in 1869, and in 1870 came the Franco-Prussian War. Napoleon III joined one of his armies, taking the Prince Imperial with him and leaving the Empress as Regent in Paris. With disaster impending at Sedan, he sent the 14 year old Prince away and the latter, shedding the uniform that his fond parents had imposed upon him, crossed into Belgium and then to England.

Meanwhile, the Emperor, on 2nd September, 1870, formally surrendered to the Prussian king. A whole army and an emperor taken captive was too much for the Parisians and they were soon hammering at the gates of the Tuileries. The Empress fled from Paris in disguise to Ryde in the Isle of Wight. From Ryde she made her way to Hastings to join the Prince Imperial. News, we are told, was brought to the Imperial family, that in the village of Chislehurst, in the County of Kent, there was a house known as Camden Place, furnished in the French style, whose owner, Mr. N.W. Strode, would make them welcome, and so, on 20th September, 1870, to Chislehurst they came.

For the first few days after the arrival of the Empress and her son, Strode shared his house and table with them, but soon moved to his other Chislehurst residence at Cranmore Place. More than one French general is said to have made his way to Camden Place during the siege of Metz, and maybe of Paris also, for Napoleon III had not abdicated and Eugenie was still Regent, but she would do nothing to impede the Government of Defence that had been set up on her departure.

The fall of the Second Empire did nothing to lessen the friendship between Eugenie and the Queen, which had originated in 1855, on a state visit to Windsor. The Empress had paid private visits to her in November, 1860, and in July, 1867, and now, on 30th November, the Queen not only came to Camden Place, but obviously pressed for a return visit to Windsor which took place five days later. The same pattern is seen in the following year. News of the Emperor's release having been conveyed to the Empress by Mr. Lord, the Chislehurst station-master, she hastily boarded a special train provided by the South Eastern Railway which took her to Dover in time to witness the enthusiastic welcome accorded to her husband on his landing on 20th March, 1871. Soon after their arrival at Camden Place, the Prince of Wales (later King Edward VII) called with an official invitation to Windsor which the Emperor visited on 27th March, 1871. Within a week, on 3rd April, Victoria paid her second visit to Camden when she was met in front of the house by the Emperor, the Prince Imperial and Prince Murat.

There can be no doubt that the Imperial family found life in exile dull after the brilliant court of the Second Empire. The Emperor brought a small personal suite with him and gave audiences on some afternoons, reserving Sundays for the notabilities, among whom were the Prime Minister, William Ewart Gladstone, Dr. Tait, Archbishop of Canterbury and, from time to time, Earl and Countess Sydney. That there were also French visitors there is no doubt for the Third Republic is said to have established spies in the Chislehurst windmill to watch their comings and goings, whilst the Emperor had a spy in the bottom of the windmill to spy upon the spies at the top. From what we know of Mr. G.H. Baskcomb, the then owner of the mill, he would have been careful to exact rent from both!

The Imperial couple walked to St. Mary's Roman Catholic Church to attend Mass each Sunday. That they occasionally watched cricket we know from the story of a magnificent catch in the outfield which Napoleon asked to be repeated for his special benefit. That they were popular with the local people we know from the parish magazine which records that their healths were drunk at the St. Nicholas' Dedication Festival in

October, 1871, when a statement was made that they had contributed generously to local charities. In the same month, Napoleon planted a cutting from a willow tree which overhung Napoleon I's former tomb at St. Helena, which cutting had been presented to him by a British Officer. Exactly where the planting took place is not certainly known, but there is a fine willow in the garden of Grantchester, Willow Grove, which was once in Camden Park and is claimed by some to be that tree.

On 20th April, 1872, Queen Victoria was again a visitor. We know from an old inhabitant who died many years ago that the Queen was enthusiastically received by the people of Chislehurst. He told us also that she insisted on bringing her own carriage, which was placed on a flat-bottomed railway truck. The royal coachman in turn insisted on occupying his proper seat so that when the train emerged from Chislehurst tunnel (longer than it is now) his face, hands and uniform were covered in soot! On 11th May, by invitation of the Emperor and Mr. Strode, the West Kent Football Club held their annual athletic meeting in Camden Park which was attended by the Emperor and the Prince Imperial who gave three of the prizes, a chronometer, a barometer and a thermometer. Music was provided by the band of the Royal Artillery.

Napoleon III died at Camden Place on 9th January, 1873. His funeral cortege on 15th January was the most spectacular up to that time seen in Chislehurst. It was headed by a deputation of Italian workmen. The hearse was drawn by eight horses caparisoned in black. The Prince Imperial walked behind, followed by the Prince Napoleon and other members of the Bonaparte family, by representatives of the British royal family and by Italian generals representing King Victor Emmanuel and the people of Italy. Then came a distinguished gathering of French marshals and generals and, finally, several thousand people of all classes. The procession across the Common took half an hour to reach St. Mary's Church where the Roman Catholic Bishop of Southwark took the service.

The Chislehurst Parish Magazine included a long obituary

extolling the virtues, but not omitting the shortcomings of the deceased monarch.

Queen Victoria, writing of Napoleon III several years earlier, reserved her opinion on his actions during his coup d'etat in 1851, but at the same time felt that he was an extraordinary man with great qualities. That she continued to hold these views is evidenced from the fact that, as a token of her friendship with Eugenie, she paid for the granite sarcophagus into which the Emperor's body was transferred on 9th January, 1874, in the mausoleum attached to St. Mary's Church which the French architect Destailleur had built at the wishes of the Empress.

It was on this occasion that Eugenie made a gift of £10 to St. Nicholas Church of England School, which it was said would be applied to the purchase of a clock. It was about this time that the same school provided the Prince Imperial with a page boy in the person of Alfred Charles Bristol, who was then about eleven years old. The Prince, who was then at the Royal Military Academy at Woolwich, took a small house nearby where Uhlmann, his valet, and Bristol, were installed.

The Prince came of age on 16th March, 1874, and what a day it must have been in Chislehurst! The railway station was gaily decorated and flew the tricolour of France, whilst in the main waiting room an inscription, wreathed in laurels and violets read "Vive le Prince Imperial 16 Mars, 1874"—and Chislehurst really meant it! An address was presented, signed on behalf of the inhabitants by Richard Whomes, who had been, up to the previous year, the landlord of "The Bull's Head".

The Prince expressed his gratitude for all the kindness that had been shown to his family since they had taken up their abode at Camden. The ladies of Chislehurst gave him "a very substantial present". About 6,000 Frenchmen, representing all the Departments of their country, gathered in two enormous marquees set up within the grounds of Camden Place within which many speeches were made with, one understands, more than one reference to Napoleon IV.

Meanwhile, Eugenie relaxed somewhat the protocol that

obtained up to her husband's death and began to pay visits to some of her Chislehurst friends, including the Wollastons at "Bishopswell".

The Prince Imperial was greatly attached to his comrades at the Royal Military Academy and pressed unsuccessfully for a commission so that he could accompany them to Zululand. Undeterred, he went as an observer, wearing a British officer's uniform without rank. Whilst on a reconnaissance from Itelezi on 1st June, 1879, the party was surprised by a small group of Zulus and the officer-in-charge fled. The girth of the Prince's horse broke and he was unable to mount. Deserted, he turned to face his attackers and, together with two troopers, was killed by assegais. When a search party found the bodies on the following day, that of the Prince was found naked, with eighteen assegai wounds, all in front—despite which a calumnious story was afterwards circulated that he died running away. The Zulus reported when interrogated after the war, that he had fought like a lion and had fired three revolver shots. They left the medals on his corpse because it was not their custom to take the ornaments from the necks of brave men who died fighting. They confirmed the flight of Lieutenant Carey and said that if the fugitives had but turned round they would have stopped their pursuit.

The particular manner of the Prince's death raised strong feeling both in England and abroad. The officer concerned was court-martialled and faced the death penalty, but the Empress, saying that this might make another widow but would not help either herself or her dead son, asked for means to be found to quash the sentence—and this was done. Meanwhile, the body was embalmed and brought to England to lie in state at Camden Place.

The funeral provided the greatest spectacle ever seen in Chislehurst. The pall bearers included Edward, Prince of Wales; his brothers, the royal Dukes of Cambridge, Connaught and Edinburgh; Prince Leopold; the Crown Prince of Sweden and Norway and the Duc de Bassano. Representatives of the French

Senate and Chamber of Deputies attended and, of course, of the Bonaparte family. Queen Victoria came to Chislehurst but stayed with the Empress at Camden Place. The gun carriage was provided and manned by the Royal Regiment of Artillery. A great concourse of people gathered on the route across the Commons, said by some authorities at the time to have been as many as 100,000. The last honours were paid by a British Army firing party outside the church.

The body of the Prince rested temporarily in St. Mary's Church whilst the stricken Empress looked for a site for a suitable resting place. She wished at first to enlarge the little Chislehurst church, but the family of its Roman Catholic founder did not wish the bodies to be disturbed. She next turned to the field adjacent, namely nearby "Hawkwood" whose owner, Mr. Joseph Edlmann, a staunch Protestant, was not prepared to sell ground for a Roman Catholic Abbey. Thus the Empress was forced to look elsewhere and eventually began the building of the fine St. Michael's Abbey at Farnborough, Hants. Chislehurst's "In Memoriam" in the parish magazine read: "He was ever ready to identify himself with matters of parochial interest and many were the little acts of charity which he quietly and unostentatiously performed . . . Long will England reverently cherish a grateful remembrance of the unfortunate young Prince, who during the years of his exile has so thoroughly identified himself with English interests and so signally gained for himself England's high opinion".

A committee, whose secretary and treasurer was Mr. T.R. Watt of "The Briars" (after whom Watts Lane is named) opened an appeal which resulted in the erection, in 1881, of the fine monument to the Prince to be seen on the Common near Prince Imperial Road. It bears his full names and, on the reverse, his Testament that he would die "with a sentiment of profound gratitude for Her Majesty the Queen of England, for all the Royal Family, and for the Country where I have received during eight years such cordial hospitality."

Another monument takes the form of a recumbent effigy

81

recessed in the south (east) wall of St. Mary's Church. The violets emblem and the golden bees of the Bonapartes are prominent on both. Queen Victoria erected a monument to the Prince in St. George's Chapel, Windsor, and the Royal Artillery Officers and Cadets erected another at the Royal Military Academy at Woolwich which their successors were careful to take with them when they removed to Sandhurst.

On leaving Chislehurst for her new abode at Farnborough Hill, Hants, in March, 1881, the Empress wrote to Earl Sydney asking him to thank in her name all those who, during her residence in Chislehurst, had shown so much sympathy in the heavy trials she had undergone. She would never forget their generous hospitality nor the touching unanimity with which the residents had raised a monument to the memory of her son. It was, the Empress concluded, with regret that she left a place of which the recollection would be always united in her heart with the sacred remembrance of those who were no more.

The bodies of the Emperor Napoleon III and of the Prince Imperial of France were removed from St. Mary's Church on 9th January, 1888, and taken with full military honours to Chislehurst railway station from whence they were conveyed by a special train to Farnborough.

Eugenie retained in her service Alfred Charles Bristol of Chislehurst who became her major domo, travelling with her through the many countries which she visited during her long life. So far as we know, her last visit to Chislehurst was on 20th October, 1890, for the funeral of Earl Sydney whose kindness during the early days of her exile she never forgot. She died in Madrid on 11th July, 1920. Her body rests, with those of her husband and son, in the crypt of the abbey which she had founded and built at Farnborough, Hants.

On the departure of the Empress from Camden Place in 1881, Mr. N.W. Strode resumed his occupancy. He died in 1890, after which the house, its contents and the park were all sold. Mr. William Willett, a builder, later to become known as the originator of Summer Time, bought part of the park, built a house for himself called "The Cedars", moved back the entrance to Camden Place and made Camden Park Road where he built six houses the initial letters of whose names were C,A,M,D,E,N. The major part of the property was vested in Camden Place Limited, in conjunction with the Chislehurst Golf Club whose links were opened by Mr. A.J. Balfour in 1894.

Several souvenirs of the Imperial days remain in the house, namely the panelling in the dining room, a fleur-de-lis fireback in the present office, the Egyptian porphyry fireplace in the billiard room thought to have been presented to the Empress at the opening of the Suez Canal in 1869, and the fine bust of her by Adam Salomon (1868), now kept on the main staircase.

A print of Camden Place in 1794.

Lord Camden.

ABOVE: The famous gates of Camden Place, 1871. BELOW: Camden Place in the same year.

ABOVE: The Emperor Napoleon III. BELOW: The monument to Marchesa Campana, (Emily Rowles) at Rome. (Courtesy H.V. Morton)

ABOVE: The Empress Eugenie. BELOW: The Prince Imperial (An original photo from Uhlmann's collection)

87

ABOVE: The Imperial Family at Camden Place. BELOW: The funeral procession of the Emperor entering St. Mary's Roman Catholic Church 1873.

88

ABOVE: The last honours following the Prince's funeral, 1879. BELOW: The Rt.
Hon. A.J. Balfour at the opening of the Chislehurst Golf Links, 1894.

THE VICTORIANS

The two outstanding figures of Victorian Chislehurst were the lord of the manor, Lord Sydney of Chislehurst, and the Rector, the Rev. F.H. Murray.

John Robert Townshend, only son of the second Viscount Sydney, was born in 1805 and succeeded to the title in 1831. He was advanced to an earldom in 1874. He was high in the favour of Queen Victoria, whom he served as a Lord-in-Waiting, Captain of the Yeomen of the Guard, Lord Chamberlain, Lord Steward and Lord Lieutenant of Kent. The arrangements fell to him for the official visit of the Emperor Napoleon III and the Empress Eugenie to Windsor Castle on their state visit on 16th April, 1855. We find him later as the link between Queen Victoria and the Empress after the latter's arrival in Chislehurst as an exile in August, 1870. The Queen paid him a visit at Frognal in 1872 when he is said to have set up the ornamental gates still to be seen there.

Lord Sydney took an active interest in local affairs including the annual cottagers' show held uninterruptedly on the Rectory Meadow from 1840 until 1914. He was one of those concerned in the building of Christ Church in 1872.

He exercised the undoubted right of the lord of the manor to sell gravel excavated on common land. This he did to such an extent that the inhabitants formed a committee under the chairmanship of the late Mr. Travers Hawes whose efforts resulted in the Chislehurst & St. Paul's Cray Commons Acts of 1886 and 1888 whereby the commons are protected from further damage and their management entrusted to a board of conservators elected at first by the Vestry and in more recent times by the Local Authority. A considerable sum was required to extinguish most of the manorial rights and this was cheerfully paid. Nature has covered up the scars and no one is now heard to complain of these excavations which went on for probably a couple of hundred years and have left us the playing pit of St. Nicholas School, the Overflow Pond (levelled by the parishioners in 1785) and the Rush Pond recently landscaped by the Conservators.

When they could, the people of Chislehurst have always fiercely resisted any encroachment upon the Commons. There is the well-known story of the old man in the late XVIIIth century asking the Lord Chancellor, Lord Camden, whether it was right to steal a goose from off the Commons. Upon receiving his lordship's uncompromising answer that such an act would be met with all the rigour of the law, the old man quietly replied "Then, m'lord, what would you say to the man who stole the common from the goose?" His lordship, who was himself at that time seeking to enclose a further strip of commons at Camden Place, was unable to reply, but the proposed enclosure did not take place. The commoners have been equally vigilant on later occasions.

Earl Sydney died at Frognal on 14th October, 1890. The late Earl's nephew, the Hon. Robert Marsham, second son of the Earl of Romney, succeeded to the manors and estates and assumed the additional surname and arms of Townshend.

The Reverend Francis Henry Murray succeeded to the living of Chislehurst in 1846 and, as we have seen, made the enlargement of the church his first task.

During the night of 15/16th March, 1857, the steeple caught fire and, being entirely of timber overlaid with wooden shingles, was speedily consumed, the bells and clock crashing to the floor in the holocaust. Some manual fire engines were brought and aided by a chain of helpers who drew 2,000 buckets of water from wells in Church Row, saved the rest of the church. It must have seemed something of a miracle, for the whole of the flaming debris fell into the interior of the building. The Rector evidently thought so, for as soon as the fire was extinguished, a Te Deum was sung by all present. From some of the sound timber that was salvaged, the parish woodwork class made two crosses, one of which was discovered, one hundred years later, serving as the altar cross on the mission ship "John Antle" on the coast of British Columbia. The other is still to be seen in the church. Within eighteen months all had been repaired. The spire is of identical height to the tower, so that when the latter was raised to make better provision for the newel stair, the spire was increased accordingly, each being 51ft. 7ins. A new ring of bells was hung and a new clock provided.

Canon Murray (he obtained his canonry in 1890) was a man of many gifts and from his early days hymnology had been one of them. In 1852, assisted by the Rev. C.R. Harrison, his former curate, he produced "A Hymnal for use in the English Church". Similarly inspired, another curate of St. Nicholas, the Rev. G.C. White, produced "Hymns & Introits" in the same year. Unlike most other churches, the Church of England has never had an official hymnal and up to the time of "Hymns Ancient & Modern" there was nothing approaching a standard work. Canon Murray set to work to remedy that deficiency.

The idea is said to have taken shape in a conversation in a railway train on the way to the west country in 1858, after which, the first formal meeting of those interested took place in the Clergy House of Murray's old friend and onetime curate, the Rev. G.C. White, at St. Barnabas, Pimlico. Thus this famous hymn book came into being and was first published as to words on Advent Sunday, 1860, and with music, on 20th March, 1861. It has been said of Hymns Ancient & Modern that "they complete, with the Book of Common Prayer and the Authorised Version of the Bible, the splendid trilogy with which the Anglican Church has endowed the English-speaking world." Few appreciate that the old Chislehurst Rectory was the place of its genesis.

The circulation of the new book, greatly to the surprise of its promoters, exceeded all expectations and soon ran into millions. The profits were thus considerable and Canon Murray applied his portion to the expansion of church life and church work in his parish so that Chislehurst owes "A. & M." a debt which it can never repay.

The first of the new churches in Chislehurst was St. John the Evangelist. The greater part of the cost was borne by Henry Berens of Sidcup Place. The original church had twin western towers and bore no resemblance to its present-day successor, now known as St. John's, Sidcup.

Canon Murray's next effort at church extension was in 1858 when he built the chapel-at-ease at Prickend that still survives in Queen's Road, although now put to other uses. Ten years later the foundation stone was laid of the Church of the Annunciation, which was consecrated by Archbishop Tait on 25th October, 1870. The altar came from the old palace of the Bishops of Rochester at Bromley (now part of Stockwell College). The east window commemorates Sub-Lieutenant H.F. Murray, lost with 500 others in the foundering of H.M.S. Captain on the night of 6th September, 1870. Only the base of the tower was then built. The Church of the Annunciation was thus the first monument to Hymns Ancient & Modern in Chislehurst. The Lady Chapel was added in 1885, and the remainder of the tower, designed by Mr. May, a churchwarden, in 1930.

Building was going on all over Chislehurst at this time. The Roman Catholic Church of St. Mary in Crown Lane had been built, mainly by the Bowden family of Coopers, in 1854. The Wesleyan Methodist Chapel (as then called) began to rise, on land given by Mr. N.W.J. Strode, in 1869, but suffered many vicissitudes. An underground stream delayed the foundations, a severe frost split the masonry and a violent gale brought down the tower just as it had been completed. All these difficulties were overcome and the church opened for worship on 5th October 1870. The congregation had previously worshipped in a building later known as Park Road Hall (by reason of which Park Road was long known as Chapel Lane). This was subsequently used for other purposes, both religious and secular, and survived until 1969 when it was pulled down to provide a car park behind the Express Dairy in the High Street.

Still remembered in Chislehurst is the story of the faithful Arab Makeppo, a native of Central Africa, known locally as George Watto, who, as a boy, was rescued from a group of slave traders by Dr. David Livingstone. He was one of those who refused to desert the dead missionary and travelled with his body all the way to the coast and then to England. He was eventually employed by Mr. Vanner, a prominent Methodist, as a gardener at "Beechcroft" and on Sundays he was the organ blower at the Methodist Church. He married a local woman, had three sons, and died aged 88.

The next church to be built in Chislehurst was at Lower Camden. On 1st June, 1871, the Bromley Record reported preparations going on for the building of a new church on the side of a hill in Camden Park and in view of the existence of the extensive caves in that vicinity, warned the builders "to ascertain that they are not undermined lest some fine morning when the spire is nearly finished the workmen may come and find the top of it just peeping out of the ground". Despite the warning, the building has survived. It was built, within the Parish of St. Nicholas, by a group of evangelical churchmen who were disturbed by the setting up of a new Roman Catholic hirearchy in England and the revival of daily worship and ritual in Chislehurst Parish Church.

The foundation stone was laid by Lord Sydney (deputising for his wife) on 10th June, 1871, and the whole work completed in little more than a year. The consecration, by Archbishop Tait, took place on 29th July, 1872. It is pleasing to note that Canon Murray attended. There was soon a need for enlargement and, surprising though it may seem, within seven years the first tower, with spire, was taken down, the nave extended and a new tower erected, after which the church was re-opened on 25th April, 1880. There was still no parish, but by Order in Council of June, 1906, a "consolidated chapelry" was instituted and a parish constituted with land ceded, by agreement, from the parishes of St. Nicholas, Chislehurst, and St. George's, Bickley. The boundaries were Chislehurst Hill, Lower Camden and Camden Park Road, plus Camden Place.

When Christ Church was built, the whole of the area north of the Old Hill was known as Raggleswood, being a part of Camden Park stretching down to what was then the Bromley boundary, at the Kyd Brook. Although the Imperial Family of France was in residence at Camden Place, the whole property was owned by Mr. N.W.J. Strode, who gave the site of the church. A short road had been driven in from Chislehurst (or the Old Hill), and the best-known of the new residents was Sir John Lubbock, the "founder" of Bank Holidays, who later became Lord Avebury. Lubbock Road was named in his honour. It was soon extended to join Lower Camden where it crosses the brook.

On the other side of the Old Hill are Mill Place and Susan Wood, set in a deep dip and at one time almost a self-contained community. Christ Church built a school here, first in a temporary building in 1874, later rebuilt in brick in 1889. Canon Murray built the Church of St.John the Baptist next to it as a Chapel of Ease to St.Nicholas in 1886. There are a general shop and two public houses, "The Imperial Arms", and "The Ramblers'Rest". The old house at the top of the hill, now "White Cottage", was a butcher's shop kept by Walter Foat, with its own slaughter house in the small yard abutting on the common at the rear. Walter remains in memory as a Q.M. Sergeant in the Chislehurst Volunteer Corps in 1915, who, having borrowed the bath in which his wife did the weekly washing, boiled simultaneously a hundred eggs for breakfast over an open fire after an overnight stay in an oast-house on a three-day route march.

The Mill Place school closed in 1907, apparently as part of the agreement setting up Christ Church as a parish. St. John's Church continued as such until 1933 when it was closed. Both buildings have since been put to commercial uses. Some old cottages that went in steps up the hill towards the watertower were demolished in 1939. They displayed a plaque portraying the windmill that once stood by the cricket ground nearby. This plaque was carefully taken down for preservation, but was smashed by children within a few minutes of reaching the ground.

Susan Wood, that is to say the narrow road and adjoining houses, seems to have been made out of the acutely sloping garden of Mr. G.H. Baskcomb who lived here until his death in 1885. He built the two stone towers or follies that stand half way down the slope, and also the spiral staircase in the chalk that leads down to the caves where he is said to have had a second kitchen garden of vegetables that will grow in the darkness.

On the top of Summer Hill (Station Hill) stood the Water Tower, from 1860 to 1963.

In 1867, Canon Murray built the Village Hall, with frontal elevation covered in split pine after the fashion of a Swiss chalet and, rather curiously, with a central fleche or spirelet. The hall immediately became the centre of social and cultural activity. It was used in inclement weather for the Sunday school treat which was otherwise held every summer in the spacious Rectory garden, orchard and hayfield.

Penny Readings were often held in the evenings and also a variety of entertainment. Not everything that was put on in the Village Hall was approved by the editor of the parish magazine. On 16th January, 1879, a negro entertainment called "Black Diamonds" was given, and next month we read: "We must express our opinion that the first song 'Kissi, Kissi' was very vulgar and not to be commended." Well, Well!

In 1878 another village hall was completed under the auspices of the Rector, this time at Prickend. It was later known as St. Mary Hall and, is being demolished. One of the first functions there was a show given by the Chislehurst Dramatic Society on 7th January, 1879 which was attended by the Prince Imperial.

The centre part of the Royal Parade was built in 1870 and was evidently given that name as a tribute to the Imperial Family of France, the Empress and her son, the Prince Imperial, having arrived at Camden Place in August of that year. Not all the inhabitants agreed with the new name, for one wrote to the parish magazine "If a name must be given, then from the usual condition of the street, Mud Row would, perhaps, be more appropriate." On the other side of the picture a local dispute came to a head during the 1880's: "Chiselhurst is famous for its dust, royalty itself having more than once remarked upon the vagrant clouds that roll in glee across its commons." And so there arose the contending factions known as "the wet bobs" and "the dry bobs". The latter wanted no increase in the rates, but the former longed for a water cart and eventually triumphed by a single vote. Stand pipes with tall rounded tops were erected at a number of cross roads and they remained a feature of the place until the tar cart ousted the water cart and dusty roads became a thing of the past.

A great deal of house building went on in the second half of the XIXth century, Chislehurst being even then, one of the favoured places within easy reach of the metropolis. The railway had reached us in 1865 (and at Bickley somewhat earlier). These were mostly large houses, standing in their own grounds, many of twenty, or thirty rooms and upwards, and many built in Kemnal Road.

Mr. G.H. Baskcomb, having successfully misnamed the old house of the Ellis's as "The Manor House", sold it to a developer who promptly opened up Manor Park (which never was a manor park) and built further houses in Manor Park Road. The Governesses' Benevolent Institution, a picturesque, much-gabled building of red brick, was built in the latter road in 1871 and survived until recently replaced by a far less elegant, but internally more comfortable building.

On the other side of Chislehurst the Viscount Walden built the house of that name that stood where now is the estate of Yester Park. He succeeded as the ninth Marquis Tweeddale in 1876, but continued to live here and died two years later. Willow Grove seems to have been carried through to join Sundridge Avenue in his time. From his title and the fact that he was born at Yester, near Edinburgh, we get the names of

Walden and Yester Roads. Dr. Oskar Teichman, in his reminis-
cences tells how Sitka, which has an entrance off Yester Road,
got its name. His father was a benevolent and well-known
local figure. He was, by trade, a fur merchant. When the
U.S.A. purchased Alaska from the Russians in 1867, all the
existing trading arrangements lapsed. At the request of the
London fur traders, Mr. Teichman senr. made a perilous journey
by steamer and sailing ship to the Alaskan capital, Sitka, where
he successfully negotiated new agreements and thus retained the
trade for Britain. The house is now occupied by the Scientific
Instruments Research Association.

The Chislehurst & Cray Valley Cottage Hospital was founded
as a result of a meeting held in St. Nicholas Schools on 1st
November, 1881. The intentions of the founders are unquestion-
able, but thousands of Chislehurst people over the ninety or
more years that have since passed, have wondered why such an
inaccessible site was chosen.

In 1881 the ubiquitous Rector of Chislehurst was in New
York, and in 1888 in Moscow. In 1889 Mr. C.V. Shadbolt, the
local aeronaut, announced that he would make an ascent in his
balloon in aid of the funds of the hospital, taking with him
Canon Murray and Mr. Hayward, editor of the District Times
(now Kentish Times). On Saturday, 18th May, the parishioners
gathered in the Rectory Meadow as Mr. Shadbolt filled up the
balloon with 40,000 cubic feet of coal gas: "quite a large order
for the Gas Company," as the local paper said. At the appointed
time the anchor was weighed and they rose quickly over
Chislehurst Common. At 3,000 ft. the aeronauts plunged into
a cloud, whereupon the Rector donned his cardigan and opened
his bottle of lemonade.

The balloonists soon found themselves over the Thames and
drifting towards London, so the valve was opened and the
balloon came down in some green fields in the Isle of Dogs
where it was mobbed by the inhabitants to obtain custom
for their horses and carts. In the ensuing fracas the envelope was
torn and the aeronauts were glad enough to be rescued by a

passing policeman. The Rector of Chislehurst subsequently hired one of the carts to take him to Canning Town. To the great relief of his parishioners, he was found in his customary seat in church next day. Cray Valley Hospital benefitted to the extent of £18. 7s. 5d.—a welcome addition to its funds, for it entirely depended on voluntary contributions.

Chislehurst has always been noted for its manifestations of loyalty to the Crown and for its capacity to organise festivities on all suitable occasions. On the golden jubilee of Queen Victoria's reign, on 21st June, 1887, the proceedings began with a service in the parish church. In the afternoon the school children assembled near the Overflow Pond and marched in procession round the village green and along Church Row "to a spot on the Common which had been selected for the planting of a jubilee scarlet oak."

The procession was led by the two bands which the village then boasted, one of brass and the other of drums and fifes under the leadership of Mr. Charles Dabner. Sports and firework displays followed, in a description of which in the parish magazine we read: "It was a decided failure owing to Mr. Pain, the pyrotechnist, having sent the set pieces which had been selected for Chislehurst to New York or some other place."

The scarlet oak flourished for a number of years near the Overflow Pond. It was surrounded by formidable iron railings, but these could not save it from destruction from a serious fire on that part of the common about fifty years after its planting.

On 24th June, 1896, amid scenes of great enthusiasm, Chislehurst celebrated the golden jubilee of Canon Murray as Rector of the parish.

For Queen Victoria's Diamond Jubilee celebrations on 22nd June, 1897, the children assembled at the various schools. A procession was then formed under the leadership of Mr. Charles Dabner and proceeded via Manor Park Road to the triangular piece of green opposite the Royal Parade where three memorial lime trees were planted, one by the Rector, and the others by the Misses Frederica Tiarks and Rachel Nussey, youngest daughters of the two churchwardens. These trees, now grown to full stature, still flourish there and are marked by a stone.

Some 1,137 medals were distributed to the children that day, and if that seems a large number it must be remembered that all the young people from the Lower Borough (Foots Cray) were brought in for the occasion. In the Village Hall there was a mammoth jubilee cake encircled with a wreath of flowers. There were again sports and fireworks on the village green and a bonfire on White Horse Hill.

For the last time in Victoria's reign, Chislehurst was en fete on 29th June, 1898, for the visit of the Duchess of Albany, the queen's daughter-in-law.

After a short service in the parish church, the Duchess drove through the streets, escorted by the local troop of the West Kent Yeomanry in their resplendent uniforms. She drove across the Commons and down the High Street to open a new road, the western half of which had just been completed on the site of the old Red Hill Farm. The eastern end, previously a cul-de-sac, was much older and had been known as Belmont Grove. There is a marked difference to be seen in the width of the street and in the type of houses in the two parts, all, since that day, known as Albany Road.

At the entrance to Camden Place and opposite "The Cedars" the newly-built house of Mr. William Willett, the 2nd. Kent Volunteer Artillery formed a guard of honour. Within Camden Park the band of the Scots Guards played while teas were served, gymnastic displays given and purses of money handed to the Duchess by a long procession of school children. The Chairman of the Fund was Sir George Chubb (later the first Lord Hayter). The Albany Institute, built with the proceeds of this day at Chislehurst, is still to be seen at Deptford.

ABOVE: Rev. Francis Henry Murray. BELOW: Chislehurst Hill, with the Rambler's Rest, c. 1807.

ABOVE: Church of the Annunciation. BELOW: The Bull's Head, 1860 (Courtesy of C.A.R. Richards)

ABOVE: Cornelius Wilson, miller of Chislehurst, and his wife, Jane, c. 1860 (Courtesy F. Pierce). BELOW: The Cricket Ground in 1871.

ABOVE: Wesleyan Chapel. BELOW: Catholic Church—both 19th century prints.

The Duchess of Albany visits Chislehurst, June 29th, 1898.

END OF AN ERA

The XXth century began with a new form of local government. The Chislehurst Urban District Council was formed in 1900, with Mr. N. Balme as its first Chairman, and with its offices in two houses at the lower end of Church Row. By some anomaly, the appointment of Commons Conservators was overlooked in the new legislation and therefore remained with the otherwise almost defunct Vestry for another 34 years. The other function of the annual Vestry Meeting was to elect the churchwardens.

King Edward VII was crowned on 9th August 1901, and Chislehurst cockpit was surrounded by miniature Venetian masts bearing wreaths of laurel connected by festoons of bunting. More than 1,000 children gathered there to sing hymns and the national anthem under the baton of Charles Dabner. Canon Murray was the chairman of the celebrations committee. It was his last public function for he fell ill shortly after and passed away, on 11th October, 1902.

Canon James E. Dawson succeeded as Rector and continued to sponsor the traditional activities of the parish. The Cottage's Show was held annually in the Rectory meadow as it had been since 1840.

Another great event in the year was Guy Fawkes Day, until at the request of the police and for the safety of the public, the Commons Conservators were forced to withdraw all facilities in 1938 and this old custom finally lapsed.

Up to the early years of this century, Chislehurst was surrounded by open country. One could go hop picking in the season and the strawberry fields at Scadbury were always thrown open to the public after the commercial picking had been completed.

50 to 60 years ago the General Post Office was in a tiny house in Church Row later known as "Teatime". The large house known as Shepherds Green (now attached to Farringtons School) was occupied by Mr. Meers who erected in it a large organ which is said to have extended from floor to roof. That organ is now in Sydney Cathedral, N.S.W., thus forming a second link between that city and Chislehurst.

In the year 1900 the South Eastern & Chatham Railway began the work of doubling the railway tracks from London to Orpington, work which entailed the provision of a second Chislehurst tunnel, which was driven through parallel to the first. Hardly had this been completed when the old tunnel began to show signs of collapse at its eastern end with the result that Chislehurst workers in the great City on 17th July, 1902, suddenly found themselves cut off from their native heath. This part of the line was entirely closed until 3rd November, by which time vast quantities of earth had been removed and the tunnel considerably shortened. In the space thus provided, Elmstead Station was built and opened in 1904. It was later renamed Elmstead Woods. Meanwhile, Chislehurst Station was rebuilt in its present spacious form.

The High Street and surrounding area is known as West Chislehurst (in contradistinction to East Chislehurst, the old name for Sidcup). Anciently it was a separate hamlet known as Prickend (with Prickyngs as a variant). The old name survives now only in the name of the pond. The oldest building is undoubtedly the Queen's Head, the centre part of which is Georgian. Its northern end, so far as the walls and roof are concerned, is much older and, up to forty years ago contained the 2-inch thick oaken vats, dating back perhaps to Stuart times, when inns brewed their own ale. These vats were removed during modernisation.

A rough book kept by Samuel Baxter, a former landlord, names a number of local inhabitants and tells us that the house was then a coaching inn. The earliest entry is for the year 1788 and the last in 1817. Another old book concerning Prickend, unfortunately since destroyed, was the account book of the Blackneys who kept the forge under the spreading chestnut tree in the High Street from 1792 onwards (where now are Barclays Bank and the London Steak House). The smithy continued under three generations of the Lash family until the 1960's. From the smithy accounts of the 1790's we have another list of local inhabitants, including Samuel Baxter, Whitby the miller, Franks the brewer, Mace the schoolmaster and others. The cost of taking down the church bells in 1805 was seven shillings.

The White Horse was another Georgian House, but after the top of the hill had been lowered in 1899 to fill the duck pond of Red Hill Farm (where now are the Library and nearby shops) the old house was pulled down and the present hotel built at a lower level. Opposite is Telegraph Path, which is now entirely hemmed in by houses but retains the oaks, hawthorns and ferns from the days when it ran across open fields. It takes its name from an Admiralty visual telegraph station that stood here from 1796 to 1822.

Recruiting for the new Territorial Army began in Chislehurst in 1908 when a local company was formed as part of the 5th Bn. The Queens Own Royal West Kent Regiment. The 1st Chislehurst Boy Scouts Troop, founded in 1908, was among the first in the country. It was followed in 1909 by the 2nd Chislehurst. In 1920, the 1st & 2nd Chislehurst Scouts combined into the Chislehurst "Invicta" Group.

On King George V's Coronation on 22nd June, 1911, the focal point of local celebrations was again the village green, Charles Dabner maintaining the lead again. There was a grand procession during which Mrs. A. Travers Hawes planted the oak that may still be seen in the village pound.

Another event of 1911 was the lighting of the church by electricity. This concession to modernity was resisted by a considerable body of parishioners who wished to retain the candles which had served them for so long. Many of the candelabra were allowed to remain, which has delighted Christmas congregations in subsequent years.

The outer world burst in on rural Chislehurst on Sunday 5th April, 1944, when the first motor omnibus arrived and service 159 began between Chalk Farm and The Bull's Head, (on Sundays only). In June of the same year, service No. 151 began to operate between Woolwich and "The Bull", but war caused these services to be withdrawn.

The years immediately preceding the outbreak of World War I saw the development of the Voluntary Aid Detachments of the St. John Ambulance and the British Red Cross, including the Chislehurst Detachment, "Kent 60".

In Chislehurst the first effects of World War I were to be seen in the visits of Army officers to all the stables in search of horses as army remounts. Batteries of artillery came from Woolwich to practice on the commons. Meanwhile, Chislehurst men were joining the regular forces. Speaking from a cart in Chislehurst High Street, Mr. H.W. Forster, M.P. for Sevenoaks (in which Division we then were) made an appeal upon which local men enlisted.

Shortly after the declaration of war, Kent 60 V.A.D. were asked to accept Belgian army casualties at short notice and forthwith fitted out Christ Church Hall as a hospital, augmenting it shortly afterwards with Abbey Lodge, an empty house in Lubbock Road, with Miss Beatrix Batten as Commandant. Miss Batten gave a lifetime to the Red Cross, became in later years County Director for Kent and received a C.B.E. from the Queen. She died in 1968. Other V.A.D. hospitals were opened in Hornbrook House, in the High Street, and in houses in Manor Park and Holbrook Lane, all of which received British and Commonwealth wounded throughout the war.

In November, 1914, the Chislehurst Volunteer Training Corps was formed, commanded by Captain Lionel J. Jackson. Only dummy rifles were used for drill purposes at first, but real rifles were available for training and .22 shooting practice took place in the loft of St. Nicholas Mens' Club and of the White

Horse stables. The Chislehurst Corps boasted a bugle band. Official recognition came in 1916 when "G.R." armlets were issued.

In 1915, Mr. H.S. Marsham-Townshend, sold the house and estate of Frognal and moved to the steward's house at Scadbury which was enlarged to take the panelling at Frognal that had originally come from the old Farringtons. Scadbury thus again became the manor house, Frognal was bought by the Government who built a large hutted hospital in the grounds which was opened in the name of the Queen's Hospital by General Sir Francis Lloyd, K.C.B., on 16th July, 1917. For many years this hospital specialised in plastic surgery and a great work was done there for those maimed and disfigured in the war. It did not become a general hospital until 1930 and is about to be superseded by a new hospital.

Chislehurst Caves, which had been chalk mines for several hundred years, were closed to the public during World War I and their extensive caverns used as storage space for explosives. The picric acid, as well as colouring the workers a yellow tint, also discoloured the chalk. A tramway was installed and continued in use until the last of the explosives had been removed. The Zeppelin raids on London, of which there were seven, began on 21st May, 1915. On those nights many Chislehurst people assembled on Telegraph Path, which at that time commanded a fine view over the bowl of London, to watch the play of the searchlights and eventually to see the airships brought down at Cuffley and Billericay.

Chislehurst had lost its new omnibus service within a few weeks of the outbreak of war. In 1916 it gained its first week-day service when No. 109 began to operate between Forest Hill and Woolwich, its prime purpose being to carry workers to and from Woolwich Arsenal. These early buses were solid-tyred single-deckers with a "cage" for the conductor at the rear. This service is now represented by the present route No. 227. Early in 1918, Chislehurst suffered from German "taube" raids, but as aeroplanes could not yet carry heavy weights, the bombs were relatively small. One fell near the Tiger's Head and, rather curiously, the hole was fenced in for some years, later to be the site of the planting of a coronation tree in 1937.

When the war ended on 11th November, 1918, those of us who returned from service overseas received an illuminated "welcome home" and gathered in the cockpit on 25th June, 1919, completely surrounded by a vast concourse of people, the hymns accompanied by a military band. Afterwards dinner was served, followed by an entertainment in a marquee in the Rectory Meadow.

Peace Day was celebrated on 19th July, 1919, with the pealing of bells, a great procession of decorated vehicles through the streets, sports in Foxbury Park and tea for all the children, including those from the Lower Borough. A tree was planted at the top of the High Street, but did not survive and was shortly replaced by the chestnut which is marked by an inscribed stone. The War Memorial at the cross roads is an exact copy of those standing in the military cemeteries of France and Flanders. It contains the names of the 186 men of that war who made the supreme sacrifice. The memorial was dedicated by Canon J.E. Dawson on 17th October, 1920.

Thus ends the local story of World War I. Chislehurst had changed, and the day of the large house, of which Chislehurst had so many, was gradually passing.

The Old White Horse, demolished 1899.

West Chislehurst: The horse pond on the site of today's Library and shops, 1875.

Mafeking Day, May 8, 1900.

ABOVE: The Fire Brigade in 1910. BELOW: Prickend National School, c. 1906.

ABOVE: The Annunciation Boys' School, Empire Day. 1914. BELOW: 121st. Heavy Battery R.G.A., on Chislehurst Common, November 1914.

ABOVE: Chislehurst Territorials in 1909. BELOW: Local lads leaving for the front, July 10, 1915.

ABOVE: Miss Beatrix Batten, C.B.E., Commandant, Kent 60 V.A.D. (Courtesy Kentish Times) BELOW: Christ Church Parish Hall as a Red Cross Hospital, October 1914.

ABOVE: Chislehurst Volunteer Training Corps, 1915. BELOW: Service of Thanksgiving for returned servicemen, 1919.

The first motorbus to reach Chislehurst (Courtesy Miss F. Cooling)

VILLAGE AT WAR & PEACE

In 1924 the Sidcup By-pass road (A20) was opened. In 1926 electricity superseded steam on all the suburban railways in N.W. Kent. In 1931, the fields to the north and east gave way to Green Way, Hill Close, Farmland Walk, Westhurst Drive, Woodside Avenue, Holmdale, Hillview and Mainridge Roads. Up to this time it was possible to walk from the White Horse Hotel to Grove Park Station across fields almost without passing a house, but soon this entire area was covered by an L.C.C. housing estate.

In 1921 Foots Cray Urban District Council had officially changed its name to Sidcup and on 1st May, 1934, merged with Chislehurst to form a single Urban District Council whose offices were at Sidcup Place and whose first Chairman was Mr. E.V. Mills. New schools were required to keep pace with the rising population and Chislehurst secured its first grammar school for girls in Beaverwood Road in 1925. The Grammar School for Boys at Crittals Corner did not follow until 1938, being later transferred to a new building in Hurst Road, Sidcup.

A considerable part of Petts Wood was bought for the National Trust under a committee chaired by Mr. H. Bird and a sundial commemorating Mr. William Willett, the originator of summer time, was unveiled by the Lord Lieutenant of Kent, the Marquess Camden, on 21st May, 1927.

In 1936, Col. F.J. Edlmann, with a few other stalwarts, founded the present branch of the British Legion.

With Britain again at war with Germany in 1939, public shelters were dug under Chislehurst Common. Chislehurst found itself just outside the great barrage of captive balloons that covered the capital. The Civil Defence Organisation in Chislehurst-Sidcup was controlled by an Emergency Committee of the Urban District Council.

A large brick-built rescue centre was erected in the Walden Open Space with road access from Ingleby Way.

The Battle of Britain, in the wonderfully fine summer and autumn of 1940, was mainly fought in the skies over Kent, with Chislehurst in the direct line from the Straits of Dover to London. On 27th September Woodcliffe Manor Hotel on Summer Hill and Ivybridge at the foot of the Old Hill were practically demolished and four people killed. During the first week in October, Mulbarton Court, in Kemnal Road was hit, the Fox and Hounds in the High Street practically demolished, the porch of the Annunciation Church shattered and several houses in Westhurst Drive destroyed. Ten people were killed in these incidents.

Immediately following the famous appeal of Mr. Anthony Eden on 14th May, 1940, a unit of the Local Defence Volunteers was formed, later to become the 54th Kent Battalion of the Home Guard, with Colonel H.W. Hill, C.M.G., D.S.O., as the mustering commander, followed in succession by Lieut. Cols. F.H. Clark, D.C.M., C.R.B. Chiesman and R. Hodder-Williams, M.C. The main defence posts were at Hawkwood, Camden Place, the building in Green Lane which is now British Legion H.Q., Scadbury and Farringtons School (then in Government hands). Road blocks were set up at strategic points and at one of these, near Holbrook on St. Paul's Cray Common, during the Battle of Britain on Sunday 18th August, 1940, a platoon of the 54th was fired on by a low-flying German Dornier aircraft whereupon, in the words of a War Office statement "They retaliated with rifle fire, and after firing 180 rounds, caused the enemy aircraft to crash. This is the first occasion on which the Home Guards have succeeded in bringing down a German bomber". The machine actually fell at Leaves Green, not far from Biggin Hill airfield.

Chislehurst also became the centre of P. Sector when Col.

F.W. Chamberlain set up his headquarters at Scadbury. The 8th (S.E.) London Group H.Q. for the whole Civil Defence Area from Penge to Erith were also in Chislehurst at Bonchester in Camden Park Road.

The night bombing which began during the Battle of Britain increased in intensity during the remainder of that year and continued in 1941 and 1942. Some of the local people and large numbers from London began to gather nightly in Chislehurst Caves where they were 120 ft. below ground. The numbers became so great that the London Regional Commissioners installed electric lighting, air conditioning and sanitary arrangements. Furniture was moved in and many who had lost their homes made this their permanent abode. In 1941, the caves became an official air raid shelter under the control of the Urban District Council. A church was set up in a large cavern and daily services held, the Bishop of Rochester being among the preachers. The caves were claimed to be the largest air-raid shelter in Britain, the number in them sometimes exceeding 15,000 people.

Chislehurst took part in the nation-wide series of Savings Weeks. One of them, Spitfire Week was in response to a county-wide appeal by the Association of Men of Kent and Kentish Men for a Kent Squadron of Spitfires, which object was duly achieved one of the machines being named "Chislehurst & Sidcup".

On 1st July, 1944, Luson House, in Willow Grove, was destroyed by a flying bomb with most of its occupants. On the 22nd of the same month six houses at the highest point in Green Lane were demolished and 30 others rendered untenable. The last of these incidents was on 29th July when St. Mary's Villas, Willow Grove, were totally destroyed and the Willow Grove and Annunciation Schools and St. Mary Hall all wrecked. The flying bombs were followed in October, 1944 by the rockets or V2s, one of which fell in Bull Lane and the last in Scadbury Park on 27th March, 1945.

The Home Guard finally "stood down" on 3rd December,

1944, the Chislehurst Battalion holding its last parade in the drive of Camden Place and then dispersed.

The war finally over, with 178 persons killed, 1,539 injured and 14,000 properties destroyed or damaged, the price of war in the Chislehurst & Sidcup Urban District had been considerable.

Saturday, 8th June, 1946, "Victory Day" saw the usual arrangements for a "Chislehurst celebration" spoilt by heavy rain. In 1951 there was a local procession as part of the Festival of Britain.

1953 was Coronation year, and celebrations were planned to last a whole week with concerts and the traditional procession on other than the date itself. For Coronation Day the author devised a special pageant, "Elizabeth and Walsingham". With the Chislehurst and the Lamorbey Park Choral Societies, the Country and Morris Dancers and the May Queens and their retinues from Chislehurst and Sidcup, the cast numbered about 250 persons, who played to an audience of 2,000 on the lawns at Sidcup Place.

At Chislehurst the poor weather did not prevent the unveiling during the afternoon of a village sign which, like the pageant, portrays the knighting of Walsingham in 1597. It has at its apex the white horse of Kent and at its base, set with mediaeval bricks from Scadbury, a tablet commemorating the coronation of the second Elizabeth. The execution of the sign was in the hands of Mr. John Easden and the cost was met by public subscription. The unveiling was performed jointly by Miss Patricia Hornsby-Smith, then Member of Parliament, straight from Westminster Abbey, and Mr.. W.G. Fuller, Chairman of the Urban District Council.

ABOVE: Opening of Petts Wood by the Marquess Camden, 1927. BELOW: The church in Chislehurst Caves during World War II. OPPOSITE: The 54th (Chislehurst) Kent Home Guard at the post from which they shot down a Dornier with 180 rifle rounds, in 1940 (Courtesy G.H. Bray)

124

ABOVE: The Fox & Hounds, virtually demolished during the Battle of Britain (October 1940). BELOW: July 1944—VI damage in Green Lane.

ABOVE: 1953 Coronation Day 'Elizabeth & Walsingham' Pageant. BELOW: Marlowe Society's Elizabeth I 400th anniversary dinner, 1958: Capt. J.P. Young and Mr. & Mrs. P. Rockliffe.

THE SHAKESPEARE MYSTERY

In 1952, Mr. Calvin Hoffman, a theatre critic, of Long Island, N.Y., U.S.A., called a press conference in London and announced to the world that a great mistake had been made inasmuch as it could be shown that Shakespeare did not write the works attributed to him. In fact, said Mr. Hoffman, they were all written by the Kentish poet and playwright, Christopher Marlowe, in hiding in the manor house of Scadbury in Chislehurst, in consequence of which the flags of all the nations should be hauled down at Stratford-upon-Avon and hoisted instead across Chislehurst Common.

The basis of Mr. Hoffman's claim is the number of parallels that occur in the works of the two authors of which he lists some hundreds, but it is well known that Shakespeare used any sources that were open to him, sometimes using, and of course, vastly improving, whole plots from other works. That he was much influenced by Marlowe, whose works immediately preceded his, is well known. In order to make Marlowe the author of the whole Shakespeare canon, Hoffman has to "undo" his death at Deptford on 30th May, 1593 and this he does by claiming that an unknown body must have been placed before the coroner's jury whilst Marlowe was secretly spirited away to live on for an unknown period of years at Scadbury, or elsewhere. This simply will not do for, as we know, his death is one of the best authenticated in all English history.

In support of his hypothesis, Mr. Hoffman conceived the notion that the works of Shakespeare, in the handwriting of Marlowe, might have been entombed with the latter's patron, Sir Thomas Walsingham, who died at Chislehurst in 1630.

He claimed that Bishop Chavasse favoured the opening of the Walsingham tomb in the Scadbury Chapel of St. Nicholas Church, but the Rector, Canon J.R. Lumb, as he had every right to do, met this request with an absolute refusal. There were those who claimed that it would be sacrilege to open the tomb, but there have been many precedents from the earliest times. Neither is Mr. Hoffman alone in searching for the lost manuscripts of Shakespeare, for individual Baconians, after deciphering secret messages from the plays, have gone a digging on the other side of the Atlantic, and in this country there was the man whose cipher told him that the manuscripts were at the bottom of the River Wye at Chepstow whereupon he employed a diver to bring them up! The diver surfaced with a Roman helmet, but no more.

Canon Lumb died in 1954 and was succeeded by the Ven. R.G.H. McCahearty, Archdeacon, who held no particular views on the subject so that when Mr. Hoffman applied again he was invited to meet the Parochial Church Council which body, after a long debate, decided to offer no objection. The lord of the manor accordingly applied for a faculty, and the matter being of some importance, a Consistory Court was held in the church on 2nd January, 1956, presided over by the Diocesan Chancellor, Mr. Percy Lamb, Q.C. The case for the applicant was put by Mr. W.G. Wigglesworth and eventually the faculty was granted under certain conditions, namely that a fully competent architect and masons should be employed and that nothing be disturbed below ground level. Mr. Wigglesworth endeavoured to obtain a ruling that anything loose found in a manor chapel was the property of the lord of the manor, a point on which the chancellor carefully declined to give an opinion.

At 10.0 a.m. on 1st May, 1956, the opening of the Walsingham tomb began under the superintendence of Lord Mottistone and Mr. Paget, Consulting Architects to the Dean & Chapter of St. Paul's Cathedral. The masons inserted a thin saw with which to remove the mortar and after about 30 minutes one half of the front of the table tomb was lifted out revealing a large quantity of sand which Lord Mottistone identified as from Caen in Normandy. No bodies were found, these being known to be in a vault below; and, of course, no manuscripts. Crowding round the church door throughout these proceedings were representatives of the world's press to whom Mr. Hoffman calmly announced the result of the morning's proceedings. This, he said, did nothing to disprove his theory, it simply eliminated another clue.

Meanwhile Shakespeare (and the Walsinghams) sleep on in peace and the flags of all the nations continue to fly at Stratford-upon-Avon.

Calvin Hoffman and his wife watch the opening of the Walsingham tomb, May 1, 1956. OPPOSITE: The tomb yields its secrets—pure sand. (Courtesy PA–Reuter)

TODAY

As the value of land in Chislehurst became greater than that of the houses upon it, the older ones came tumbling down to give place to a number of smaller dwelling set in the former spacious gardens. The old Rectory, built in 1735, was pulled down in 1960, being in a state of disrepair after requisition and the present Rectory was built immediately behind the old. The stables, orchard and meadow gave way to the present Bishops Way and The Glebe. About this time also, Holbrook and Hawkwood gave way to modern replacements. Since then, Heatherbank, on Summerhill, Old Hill House, and other large buildings have followed.

In May, 1963, amidst a storm of controversy, the Water Tower was demolished. It had stood astride the top of Summerhill since 1860 and, although erected by Mr. George Wythes, of Bickley, as the entrance to his estate, it had come to be regarded as the gateway to Chislehurst. Great efforts were made to preserve it, but a majority of the members of the Chislehurst & Sidcup Urban District Council voted that it should come down. A meeting of Chislehurst Residents Association held in that same week, sent a final petition by telegram to the Minister of Housing and Local Government praying that Chislehurst be separated from Sidcup, on the last day of the parliamentary debate on the London Government Bill. The Minister agreed and the Bill was amended so that Chislehurst became part of Borough 19 (Bromley) instead of Borough 18 (Bexley) as first planned. This, on 1st April, 1965, marked the end of the Chislehurst & Sidcup Urban District Council. Wythes' arms, carved in stone on the Water Tower, were preserved with the intention that they be incorporated in a public seat on the site, but the Borough declined to meet the cost and insufficient money having been collected by the Residents Association, the matter remains in abeyance. As to the new boundary, common sense dictated that it be drawn on the line of the A20 road, so that Frognal and the whole of the former Lower Borough are now in the Borough of Bexley.

A number of centenaries loomed up in 1970 and the immediately following years. In 1970 an ad hoc committee arranged a commemoration of the coming to Chislehurst of the Empress of France and the Prince Imperial 100 years earlier. A number of distinguished guests, mostly members of the Souvenir Napoleonien on 19th August, attended a service in St. Mary's R.C. Church and were then officially welcomed at the Prince Imperial Monument by the Mayor of Bromley, Alderman Miss Bertha James, J.P. The Prince Murat replied on behalf of the visitors. Other centenaries commemorated were those of the opening of the Annunciation and Methodist Churches (1970) and Christ Church (1972). In January, 1973, a party of Les Amis des Napoleon III visited Camden Place in connection with the centenary of the death of the Emperor.

In May, 1973, came the golden jubilee of the present series of Chislehurst May Queens whose crowning on the Common above Prickend Pond (with the sole exception of 1942) has taken place annually. The May Queen in the Jubilee Year was Wendy Shefford who was greeted by Mrs. F. Armstrong nee Everist, the May Queen of 1923. The current year's queen is Carol-Ann Sells.

Thanks to its Commons and to the unremitting efforts of its citizens, Chislehurst has managed to keep its outward appearance more or less unchanged, but this is being sharply assailed in 1974 when a comparatively large area of the High Street has been demolished and levelled for redevelopment, so far disallowed, and shortly the subject of a public enquiry. The High Street is part of a Conservation Area.

An unusual event occurred on 26th January, 1974, when

Mr. C.M. Pankhurst, of North London, detected silver coins on the commons between the Rush Pond and Centre Common Road, about 3 feet down. There were 307 florins and half crowns, most of them in mint condition, dating from 1848 to 1917, with an estimated market value of £4,000. The hoard is thought to have been buried by someone during World War I. At a Coroner's inquest held on 29th May, the find was declared to be treasure trove, the property of the crown, but the coins were later returned to the finder.

To close on the theme of Imperial Chislehurst, the Academie du Second Empire is about to visit Camden Place to affix a plaque commemorating the Imperial stay.

Appropriately, perhaps, this history of Chislehurst appears just one thousand years after the earliest known mention of our place-name in King Edgar's charter of A.D. 974. It is to be hoped that, whilst loyal to the London Borough of Bromley, Chislehurst will retain its identity and traditions for the centuries still to come.

NOTE TO 1980 IMPRESSION

Some of the late author's modern references were overtaken by 1980. Following a fire in 1975, the Jacobean panelling had gone at Scadbury (page 36). The International (63) had gone; St Mary Hall (96) had been demolished and the London Steak House (108) replaced by another restaurant. Carol-Ann Sells was May Queen in 1974, and the redevelopment that was then disallowed and subject to a public enquiry, was permitted after all, and was nearly complete in November 1980; it incorporated a new Sainsbury supermarket with offices above. The plaque was duly affixed on 1 November 1974.

NOTE TO 1997 EDITION

The Ministry of Defence site is now a Muslim School (page 34) and the banana distribution centre a wood merchant's (35); John Allen became Rector in 1979 (44) and St Michael's Orphanage is a residential complex (51). While the Village Hall (56) was burnt down but rebuilt, the Co-op has gone for good (63). The seat came and went too, thanks to vandals, though the coat of arms remains (66) and Shepherds Green is no longer attached (107) to what is now Farrington's Stratford House School; the White Horse was inexplicably mechanised as the Pennyfarthing (108) and the (Queen Mary's) Hospital was built (110), though the 227 'bus service was deconstructed. Last but not least, Scadbury was bought by Bromley Borough, and is a public open space – the moated hall was exported to the Weald and Downland Museum in Sussex. Ichabod – the glory has departed. CB

The crowning of the May Queen—ten years ago. Miss Heather Shepherd, now Mrs. T. McLeod (Courtesy Kentish Times)

Prickend Pond and High Street, Chislehurst—today (Courtesy A.W.J. Scroggs)

BIBLIOGRAPHY

Annals of the West Kent Cricket Club, 1812–1896	Philip Norman	1896
Bromley Record, The		1870's
Chislehurst Parish Church (booklet)	T.A. Bushell	1972
Chislehurst Parish Magazine, from 1867 onwards		
Chislehurst and St. Paul's Cray Commons	T.A. Bushell, C.L. Platt & F.J. Holroyde	1970
Chislehurst Vestry Books, from 1752 onwards		
Christ Church, Chislehurst, 1872–1972	E.N. Parker	1972
Death of Christopher Marlowe	J. Leslie Hotson	1925
Empress Eugenie	Harold Kurtz	1964
Fall of the Third Napoleon	Theo. Aronson	1970
Golden Bees, The	Theo. Aronson	1964
Guide to the Churches of Chislehurst, A	E.A. Webb	1901
History of Chislehurst, The	E.A. Webb, G.W. Miller, J. Beckwith	1899
Intimate Memoirs of Napoleon III	Baron D'Ambes	—
Man Who Was Shakespeare, The	Calvin Hoffman	1955
Napoleon III	Graham Brooke	1933
Napoleon III in England	Ivor Guest	1952
Napoleon III and the Women He Loved	H. Fleischmann	—
Patchwork of the History of Chislehurst	Dorothy McCall	1963
Prince Imperial, The	Katherine John	1939
Prince Imperial, Le	Augustin Filon	1912
Second Empire, The	Philip Guedalla	1922
Tragicall History of Christopher Marlowe, The	J.E. Bakeless	1942
A Traveller in Rome	H.V. Morton	—
Trois Mois Chez les Zoulous	Paul Delage	1880
True Story of the Empress Eugenie, The	Count de Soissons,	1921
Washing of the Spears, The	D.R. Morris	1966
Wood on the Stony Hill (St. Mary's R.C. Church Chislehurst)	Rev. T.P. O'Beirne	—
One Dagger for Two	Philip Lindsay	1932
The Chislehurst Mystery	E.L. Mann	1938
The Return of Sherlock Holmes—"The Abbey Grange"	A. Conan Doyle	—

INDEX TO PERSONAL NAMES

138

ABOVE LEFT: Louis Napoleon as he was when he met Emily Rowles and RIGHT: in his final year as the exiled Emperor Napoleon III. BELOW LEFT: the young Prince Imperial when first exiled and RIGHT: in his Woolwich Artillery uniform, the Prince that Chislehurst mourned. (Mansell Collection)

ENDPAPERS: FRONT- The drawing room at Camden Place in 1871 and BACK - the room there where the Emperor died in 1873. (Mansell Collection)